G R E E N L A N D

Devon I.

Str. Beechey I. Lancaster Sound

merset I.

BAFFIN

BAY

Pt. Regent Inlet

Gulf of Boothia

Victoria Har.

BAFFIN ISLAND

Fury and Hecla Strait

Lord Mayor B.

Foxe

Basin

Committee Bay

DAVIS STRAIT

Foxe

Channel

Wager Bay

Southampton I.

Roes Welcome Sd.

Frobisher Bay

Resolution I.

erfield let

Hudson   Strait

Digges Is. C. Woolstenholme

Marble I.

Cape Chidley

Mansel I.

Ungava

Bay

H U D S O N

ce of Wales Churchill

BAY

Severn Fort

C. Henrietta Maria

James

Bay

Albany Ft.

Charlton I.

Ruperts R.

Moose Ft.

Pt. Comfort

Nottaway R.

ICEBOUND

Journeys to the Northwest Sea

ABOUT THE BOOK

This sympathetic and beautifully written book recreates the personal integrity and obsessive determination of those men who searched and found the icebound route between Europe and the Orient.

Like the conquest of Everest or the conquest of the moon, the conquest of the Arctic remains one of the most remarkable stories of man's defiance of the impossible. For 00 years men braved this frozen world—from Cabot, Hudson and Baffin to Parry and Franklin. This is the story of the great collective drive on a superhuman scale which has so enriched our knowledge of ourselves and the world we live in.

Drawing on his own experience of Arctic conditions, James Scott, himself a veteran Arctic explorer, describes the exhilaration of his predecessors' death-defying exploits; the blizzards, the gales, the mounting up of ice pack, the problems of transport, food supply and frostbite, mirages in the snowy wilderness.

ABOUT THE AUTHOR

J. M. Scott was born in 1906 and educated at Cambridge University. He began his career as an explorer in Labrador and Greenland, experience which he put to good use in the War as commandant of a winter warfare training school. He has devoted most of his career to journalism and has written more than 20 books of which his novels *Seawyf* and *Heather Mary* have been outstandingly successful, as have his books *The White Poppy* on the opium trade and *The Great Tea Venture*.

ICEBOUND

Journeys to the Northwest Sea

J. M. Scott

GORDON & CREMONESI

Designed by Heather Gordon

Set in 12 on 13pt Garamond
by Preface Ltd, Salisbury
and printed in Great Britain by
The Garden City Press Ltd,
Letchworth, Herts.

British Library / Library of Congress
Cataloguing in Publication Data

Scott, James Maurice
Icebound
1. Arctic regions
I. Title
919.8′04   G620   77-30053

ISBN 0-86033-018-4

Gordon & Cremonesi Publishers
New River House
34 Seymour Road
London N8 0BE

Contents

Chapter 1

The Scene

Anyone who has been in the Arctic faces the question, "What is it like?" This is no more easy to answer in a few words than would be a question, addressed to a resident of the Arctic back from a visit to Europe, of what Europe is "like". Indeed, Europe covers a considerably smaller area than does the Arctic and is far more clearly defined.

The Arctic has no definite boundaries. On a map, the only indication of where it begins is a dotted line in latitude 66° 32′ — calculated by southern Europeans 2,000 years ago. Arktos, the Great Bear, orbits the Pole Star in that latitude of the heavens and is always above the horizon in the northern hemisphere.

The dotted line does not cage all that we think of as arctic lands. Greenland projects a long way through it. The whole of Iceland is south of the circle. But, in general, arctic conditions begin near the Arctic Circle. The tourist who drives northwards by the inland roads of Norway (leaving the rocky coast to his left) may pass within hours from luxurious forests of pine and spruce to a zone where conifers are as rare as hairs on a balding head and birches and willows crouch in rocky gullies. Moss and lichen are the main vegetation and there are extensive bogs, because the melted snow is held only a foot or two down by rock-hard permanently frozen earth. This is the tundra, the threshold of the Arctic, and beyond it lies the ocean that caps the world.

Throughout the whole northern coastline of Asia and the first half of that of America the dotted line fences off the forest (more or less). But east of that, as it enters much the most varied and complex segment of the North, the line completely loses its usefulness as a boundary. The coastline, which west of here is comparatively straightforward, now becomes deeply indented; instead of few and well separated offshore islands, there is more land than water, a tortuous maze extending almost to the Pole; west to east the topography changes from the sandy delta of the Mackenzie river, the discoverer of which did not recognize the sea when he saw it, to Greenland's icy plateau; and the boundary of arctic vegetation — or lack of vegetation — drops southwards to England's temperate latitude. This is a very large segment of the Arctic, yet it is not too big for one who has travelled in it to say what it is like. It is the scene of this story. The theme is how men tried to get through it to reach the Orient.

The North-West Passage appears quite straightforward on a modern map. The wide and obvious entrance is between Greenland and Labrador. This for convenience we shall call the Forecourt. Greenland gives one an idea of what northern Europe must have been like in the Ice Age. It is a mountainous country, but only about a tenth of its land surface is exposed, the rest being covered by permanent ice, consolidated snow, which throughout the ages has piled up to eight or nine thousand feet. The pile cannot grow higher because the coastal mountains cannot contain any more snow and ice — as a plate can hold only so much sugar — and glaciers leak slowly out by the valleys. Also the wind scalps the still granulated surface. At the equinoxes and in winter there are tremendous storms. A wind-gauge that was set up on the east coast by a party I was with registered 120 miles per hour before it blew away. In such conditions it is difficult to breathe, not only because of the pressure, but also because the air is as turbid as in a sandstorm.

When snow is very cold it is as dry as sand. The ice cap itself has an undulating desert surface. For this reason, when you cross Greenland, and although in general you are climbing all the way till you reach the centre, the coastal mountains soon drop below the horizon. Thereafter, until the summits that fringe the opposite coast gradually appear, there is nothing except the desert of snow. Yet there is beauty of light in summer, as when the sun dips towards the white horizon lighting the clouds for sunset and then fans the same embers to kindle dawn.

The coast is more deeply indented with fjords than is that of Norway. At the heads of these long inlets are cliffs of ice, the glacier faces, the frozen river mouths. Pressed gradually forward, huge pieces break off—calve—and float away as icebergs.

Imagine gems the size of castles but of fantastic shapes floating in blue water, reflected in it, with all the tricks of translucency. Sometimes it is absolutely calm and silent; the sunlight gives the colours of fairyland, and black rocks are the background. Vary the scene and imagine the sheltered hollows that occur, where in the brief spring–summer thousands of flowers bloom.

The west coast of Greenland is more sheltered than the east and possesses more ice-free ground. Across about 500 miles of sea (the Forecourt) it faces Labrador, and, at rather less, what the old voyagers and cosmographers called the broken lands—the maze of islands. Only in the most northerly of these are there plateaux of permanent ice, and therefore glaciers. The scenery is majestic, wild, and for the most part monochrome, except in summer (the only season when the early voyagers ventured there), when the sea is blue and dotted with ice floes and flowers bloom in the sheltered valleys. The coastline is so deeply indented that the first explorers experienced great difficulty in telling a bay from a strait, and *vice versa*.

Labrador, of course, is part of continental America. Its northern part is bare and rocky, arctic in climate, flora and fauna—though far below the dotted line. Its southern part is thickly forested with spruce. This area is arctic only in the intensity of its winter cold, and is in the same latitude as central England.

The indented coastline stretching northwards from Labrador, and lying between, roughly, latitudes 55° and 75° North (1,200 nautical miles), was, then, the barrier through which the searchers for the North-West Passage tried to find a way. They did not believe that the barrier was as great as it proved; but, even if they had been fully informed as to which indentations were channels and which were landlocked bays, they would have found enormous difficulty in getting through.

The reason is that the Arctic consists not only of land and water but also of drifting ice. This is something quite different from the stuff that forms on lakes and ponds and can be walked over. Drifting ice consists of fragments of sea ice—floes—some formed the winter before but most being several years old. Occasionally they are piled together by storms. Floes are as unsymmetrical as jigsaw pieces, and may be as small as a table or as extensive as a large park. They are formed as follows.

The sea freezes several feet thick in a single winter. The salt water first granulates, achieving a consistency something like that of a rice pudding, then coagulates and solidifies. It is as white as snow and looks as soft, but is as hard as the freshwater ice that a sharp skate-edge scarcely scratches. (I once jumped from a ship's bow onto the "snow", and raised a bruise the size of half a rugger ball.) The vast winter icefield—not smooth, of course, for old floes tilted at all angles are imprisoned in it—is thinned slightly by the summer thaw, fragmented by the restless water below, and shattered by storms and waves. Then wind and currents disperse or herd the floes.

The effect of wind is local and varied: currents set the general pattern. The Gulf Stream reaches Norway's North Cape with just enough strength left to stir the Polar Ocean and prevent the drift ice from approaching Scotland. Ice from the Siberian coast is carried over the top of the world. As water has flowed into this almost-enclosed ocean, water and the ice it carries must flow out. Little escapes through Bering Strait, between Asia and America, for there strong tides vacillate. A great deal of ice is carried south by the East Greenland current to sweep past Labrador and even Newfoundland. (The *Titanic* was sunk by an iceberg at a point much nearer to the Equator than to the Pole.) And ice sieves through the maze of islands west of Greenland, more or less blocking the sieve—and therefore the North-West Passage—over an area more than a thousand miles square. That is why the sailing-ship explorers would have needed a lucky season or more to reach the Pacific from the Atlantic, even if they had known the way.

Drift ice has a devilment all its own. It can obstruct a ship as effectively as land does, yet it cannot be mapped. It may be here one season and gone the next; it sometimes concentrates or disperses within a day. It can imprison and crush—it often has—like the nightmare of land closing in upon a ship. A conglomeration of floes with or without icebergs added to the mixture is called pack ice, or, more briefly, the pack. It is an apt word—a pack of wolves in sheep's clothing. When the floes are set in motion by a storm and grind together, the noise is terrifying; but, when it is calm, no flock could graze more peacefully.

Because of its devilment one can do little more than generalize about drift ice. (Firm ice—the thing we all know—goes when the temperature rises; drift ice hangs about as long as it likes wherever it likes.) But there are a few guidelines. A ship caught far from land—in the full force of the pack—is lucky if it escapes being crushed. If caught among islands (as in the Arctic archipelago) and not thrust against rocks, it has a good chance of getting out, eventually—the more sheltered the harbour, the longer it may take. What sort of progress a ship can make among the islands is largely the luck of the season—or depends on factors that we still do not know. Far from land the currents give a pretty good guide, at least to the no-go areas. The pack is always very heavy between north-east Greenland and Spitsbergen and for some distance further east—the approach to the Pole. We have been thinking here in terms of sailing ships, but modern technology has not helped much, at least on the surface. To put it in Irish, no one has sailed over the North Pole without going under it.

What is life like in these regions? The sea is full of tiny creatures and therefore there are plenty of fish. I cannot remember exactly what I paid for the ton of halibut I once bought to feed my hundred huskies, but is was not much more than a housewife spends in a supermarket on a Saturday morning. Whales, seals, walruses and polar bears feed well enough. So do the land animals, foxes and caribou, which have a taste for moss and lichen. So, apparently, do insects, during their brief summer lives, though this does not prevent them from making the most of the ocassional man. Millions of ducks and geese and certain sea birds fly to the Arctic every year, so presumably they find it worthwhile.

If other animals can live with apparent comfort in the Arctic, why should not men? They do. Eskimos, the aborigines of our sector, have done so throughout historical times. There is no evidence that they were driven north by conquerors. Being nomadic hunters, they were always on the move and gradually spread eastwards from Asia until the Atlantic stopped them. Some of them diverged a long way north, among the maze of islands and along the Greenland coast. But they never turned south, even in empty country, of which there was plenty. The presumption is that they found the Arctic to their taste.

The early searchers for the North-West Passage did not. They found both the Arctic and its people very strange and unattractive. "As the Country is barren and unfertile, so are they [the Eskimos] rude and of no capacitie to culture", wrote a sixteenth-century chronicler. They were savages, infidels, even cannibals—they had to be to live in such a locality. Frobisher's men stripped off the boots of an ugly old woman to see if she had cloven feet. They knew the Arctic only in summer, yet were so awed by it that they were continually calling upon God for help—albeit that they showed few other signs of religious conviction.

Having roughly defined our area—Greenland and the islands of the Canadian Arctic—we need to examine from a more objective point of view than that of the early voyagers what life is like there. This means looking at the Arctic from the point of view of its permanent inhabitants, the Eskimos.

The Arctic is a land of feast and famine. There would be little of the latter if the Eskimos, who have no religion of their own (apart from taboos), did not stick to the Christian injunction of taking no thought for the morrow. Although they have every opportunity for cold storage, they eat to the point of bursting or go hungry. They are, however, skilful hunters, and their ability for getting about is remarkable.

Snow, as skiers have recently discovered, makes a wonderful travelling surface. Also, in one of its many conditions, it is first-class building material with good insulating qualities. Ice enables you to walk on water. When there is no firm ice but a lot of drift ice, the small, light, highly manoeuvrable kayak is ideal. Ashore it can be carried by hand or on a sledge, and dogpower is more reliable than horsepower. The Eskimos did not invent the wheel because it would not have been useful to them.

They invented numerous things that are useful: a lathe-like apparatus that makes fire by friction-generated heat; a great variety of ingenious hunting instruments; bone needles; sinew thread; and a lamp that melts out its own oil from blubber and so is always full.

Arctic as an adjective is synonymous with cold. Yet you never see a cold Eskimo. The Eskimo eats the right food and wears suitable clothes; he has learned to adapt. He does not lie down in the snow and die: he lies down in well-made snow shelters and is comfortable.

The Eskimos were living astride the North-West Passage throughout the four centuries of the search. If they had been persuaded to do so, they could have harnessed up their dogs, loaded their kayaks and oomiaks (bigger skin boats for women and children) and found the way. But to depend upon, and particularly to learn from, primitive people is a sign of humility, which (except before God) is not characteristic of explorers, who issue a challenge to indifferent Nature. Therefore, particularly in the early days, they treated the Eskimos as dangerous.

They were not dangerous. But neither were they helpful, unless suitably encouraged, and supervised. Being as pure communists as the early Christians they shared everything except their clothing and hunting instruments. (Until they were taught Christianity they shared their wives.) They did not comprehend the verb "to steal". Also they had the mentality of a crowd round a street accident: interested but unwilling to get involved. In an incident recorded later in this book, they watched fifty white men die and then took their possessions. They watched the Franklin survivors trailing slowly to their deaths, and then rifled their caches. They were never exemplary characters; but they know how to live and travel in the Arctic, which the explorers from Europe did not.

The explorers found things out the hard way on their own. Not until the nineteenth century did white men learn anything from the Eskimos. Not until the end of the search for the Passage did they drive dogs themselves. They never used a kayak. Yet these accomplishments are no more difficult than driving a horse and trap or riding a bicycle. But, oh, the exhilaration of attempting either! It means laying aside all one's educational superiority and becoming practical.

That is the point. It took a long time to chart the North-West Passage. It did so because it took so long for the explorers to achieve the state of mind that would have made it comparatively easy. Anyone can explore, when he has to, whatever his character and dreams. Individuals do it well or badly, quickly or slowly, but it is a job like any other. The frequently-asked question of why men choose to explore suggests that the motive is always the same; but the truth is that it varies from person to person, as persons vary.

Explorers are alike only in that they explore of their own free will. It is not necessarily a lifetime's occupation, but a reputation as an explorer sticks for life. You cannot divide the world into explorers and non-explorers, but, clearly, there are certain people who would explore if the chance offered, and those who would not. The reader of a book of this sort is probably in the first category, and as such will know his own motive at least.

Chapter 2

The Stream of Imagination

We must search a long way back to find the source of the river of dreams and dangerous endeavours called the North-West Passage. It cannot be said to derive from a single spring: there are many of comparable importance. So we must explore the whole catchment area through which flow—first underground, then on the surface—all the waters that converge to make the stream large enough to be definitely identifiable and worthy of a name—a name it carries all the way, through stretches rapid and powerful or almost stagnant until at last it reaches the sea for which it is destined.

Marco Polo was the first European to describe the Orient at first hand. Previously Europeans knew only what the Crusaders (whose experiences were limited) had reported, and what the Bible said. From the East had come the Three Wise Men bearing gifts of gold and myrrh and frankincense. Such things rich and rare, and silks and spices also, still reached Europe, thus linking legend with reality. In medieval times they were picked up by Venetian merchant ships in the Levant, at the terminals of the Asiatic caravan routes, or at Alexandria, which (by camel and the Nile) was the entrepot for goods brought up the Red Sea from the Indian Ocean and beyond. But how could any man know anything positive of this?

In 1271 Marco Polo, at the age of seventeen, set out with his father and uncle, rich merchants of Venice, who were making a second visit to Cathay (that is, China). They sailed to the Palestinian port of Acre, then travelled overland. They visited trading towns now buried by sand, crossed the salt desert of Kerman, the Pamir mountains and the Gobi desert until at last they reached Peking. The journey had taken them three and a half years.

There the Great Khan Kublia was much impressed by Marco's spirit and intelligence. When the young man had learned the language, he was sent to report on distant provinces and states; and in due course he accumulated a great amount of information (some at first hand, some by hearsay) about the East, its riches and its customs.

Soon after his return to Venice, in 1295, Marco Polo became involved in a war between Venice and Genoa and was captured in a sea fight. During his imprisonment in Genoa, he told his story to a fellow prisoner, Rustichello, who wrote it down. The result was a medieval bestseller (that is, among those who could read), and, though few believed all that Marco had to say, the work swung the compass of imagination to the East. Gradually the word spread; stories were retailed; and the Venetian sailors and merchants who brought oriental luxuries to Southampton, in exchange for English wool, brought their stories with them to England.

English merchants were interested, but the trade with the East was virtually the monopoly of Venice, which was then the dominant seapower in the Mediterranean and had commercial arrangements in the ports at the end of the caravan routes. Venice's monopoly of the trade continued until the sixteenth century, which was when England's star began to rise.

Before that, England was in no way a maritime power, and her ships rarely ventured far out of home waters. Her principal exchange commodity was wool, for which she was renowned, and the wool business had a strong influence on the English way of life—as can be seen from the many still-current phrases that hark back to it. Scholars with fine-drawn features follow the thread of their discourses, unravelling mysteries of life. Lawyers try to pull the wool over each other's eyes, and the Lord Chancellor sits on the Woolsack. Sailors and other homespun men spin a yarn, tease a fellow about the spinster with whom he is in love, or go woolgathering in daydreams.

It was, nonetheless, on the pastures of England that the battle of the seas was begun. The men who carried the wool cleared the Channel of pirates long before there was a Royal Navy, and sometimes took their cargoes further or engaged in piracy themselves. Gradually the search for new markets led traders further and further afield, and thus mariners increased in skill.

Another point of subsequent importance is that the English gentry had a habit, which seemed to continentals heartless, of sending younger sons away from their comfortable homes to work. They became apprentices and in some trades sailed the seas. As juniors they manned the ropes. They learned to use their hands as well as their inherited authority.

With the first Tudor king something strong enough to be called a navy was created; but its purpose was the policing of home waters, and merchantmen ventured further at their own risk. However, that there were bold spirits ready to venture was proved by the fishermen of the age, who, in search of herrings, were drawn out into the North Sea, and, in search of cod, sailed into Icelandic waters and, later, to the banks of Newfoundland. Quite possibly they discovered America—after the Vikings but long before Columbus. They were the first true English explorers, but they left no written record of their discoveries.

Other seamen, who carried cargoes that were not their own, could go only where they were told. The merchants were not so rash as to send their cloth unlabelled, as it were, to unknown places. Not, that is, that they were uninterested in new markets and sources of supply; but they were first and foremost level-headed men of business.

From the second decade of the fifteenth century, Portugal began to emerge as the dominant maritime nation in Europe. Seeking first to destroy the power of the Moors in North Africa, the Portuguese gradually ventured further. Prince Henry the Navigator, who had in full measure the inquiring spirit of the Renaissance, sent his captains exploring down the west coast of Africa. They navigated almost entirely by dead reckoning, by the mariner's compass, but as they gained experience began to learn about the constant winds and currents that rule the southern seas.

Without this knowledge, or means of recording it as it came, a sailing ship works the ocean much as a spaniel does a field. So Madeira and Azores were discovered, or rediscovered, the Guinea coast was opened up and Cape Verde rounded. By the middle of the century the Portuguese were nearly halfway down Africa, trading and colonizing as they progressed but not yet with any thoughts of finding a sea route to India.

Meanwhile spices and other oriental products continued to travel west by the age-old caravan routes to the Levant or by ship to the head of the Red Sea, for transhipment to Alexandria. Once they had reached the Mediterranean, the Venetians picked them up and carried them west. By then they were extremely expensive, for duty had to be paid on them to every ruler on whose land they touched or through whose territory they passed. The trade, however, was highly organized and there seemed no reason why it should not continue flowing along the same routes for ever. There appeared to be no alternative.

In 1462, two years after the death of Prince Henry of Portugal, Ptolemy's map of the world was published. This map, dating from the second century AD, showed the world as a sphere, and its publication had an important influence on fifteenth-century mapmaking. Thirty years later, Columbus sailed west in an attempt to find a short route to the Indies. He discovered America instead, but the Flattists' days were numbered.

Columbus cannot have been the only person to whom it occurred that the world was round, and that, as a logical deduction, the Indies could be reached by sailing westward. He was the one to gain the patronage to put the theory to the test; but there must have been may sailors who had noticed that the first part of an approaching ship to appear above the horizon is its mast, which, conversely, is last part of it to be visible as it disappears from sight. For such men it required no great effort of the intellect to believe that the world was spherical; yet it was not given to every man to surmount superstition and doggedly pursue the idea, as Columbus did. Portugal, France, and the England of Henry VII declined to patronize him, but eventually the Genoese sailor found a willing sponsor in Isabella of Spain, who talked her husband, Ferdinand, into backing Columbus. The result was the discovery of the New World, and within fifty years the Aztec and Inca empires had been conquered and Spain was firmly established in her new dominions.

During this same period, it became clear that America was not Cathay, Vasco da Gama discovered the sea route to India by way of the Cape of Good Hope, and Magellan succeeded in reaching the East by way of the Straits of Magellan, at the southern end of South America. These events put an end to the Venetian monopoly of trade with the Orient; but, from the point of view of England, the routes they opened up were very roundabout indeed. With the Panamanian isthmus and the rest of central America under the control of Spain, there was no short-cut to be had in that area; and there was no simple equivalent in the other direction. In view of this, and England's growing maritime prowess, it was only natural that the possibility of a route round the top of the world began to seem more and more worth the investigation.

Chapter 3

What Happened to John Cabot?

The exploits of John and Sebastian Cabot mark the beginning of England's search for what later became known as the North-West Passage to Cathay. As such they deserve the documentation due to pioneers.

The trouble is that we do not know in any detail what they did. A number of books have been written about them, assessing the evidence so far brought to light; but there are so many blanks, uncertainties and downright contradictions in the information available to us that it is impossible to treat the subject properly in less than full scope. As a result, whenever the Cabots are mentioned in a general history, as they have to be, it is on so small a scale that the gaps and doubts are not evident. We must try to strike a mean, giving father and son something like the space that their importance deserves, even if it means using deduction where documentary proof is lacking.

Giovanni Caboto (his name is variously spelt) was a Genoese who obtained Venetian citizenship by maintaining residence in the republic for the stipulated period of fifteen years. In about 1495 he brought his family to England, "having occasion to resort thither for trade of merchandise, as is the manner of the Venetians to leave no part of the world unsearched to obtain riches". This is the motive attributed by Peter Martyr of Angleria, who was a personal friend of John's son Sebastian.

John Cabot was an exceptionally enterprising merchant, imaginative and well educated. He was also a cartographer and globe-maker (he constructed at least one globe); he studied Marco Polo; and in 1483–4 he visited Alexandria and Mecca and inquired into the means by which the spices of the East arrived by land and sea. Almost certainly it was then that it occurred to him that a more practical trade route might be opened by sailing west.

There is no evidence that Cabot put forward the project in his native Venice. He visited Portugal and Spain. But Columbus was ahead of him with a similar plan, which had been rejected in Lisbon and was shortly to be adopted in Seville. Cabot may still have been in Spain when Columbus returned in 1493—to set out again within three months, still acclaimed as the discoverer of the western sea route to Cathay.

Cabot must have been among the first to doubt this claim. We have no way of knowing how soon he came to assess the evidence, though he must certainly have wondered about the comparative shortness of Columbus's voyage west, and about the disparity between Columbus's descriptions of a passive, primitive population and Marco Polo's descriptions of the advanced civilization of Cathay (in about the same latitude as the West Indies). It was owing to considerations such as these that Cabot modified his original plan for a voyage launching into the Atlantic through the Straits of Gibraltar or from Portugal, and instead looked to England as a starting point. He brought his family to England and in 1495 rented a house in St Nicholas Street, Bristol, at forty shillings a year.

He went to London and solicited Henry VII for his patronage. So effectively did he do this that the Milanese ambassador reported to his duke, "He tells all this in such a way, and makes everything so plain, that I also feel compelled to believe him." He added that Cabot was "of kindly wit and an expert mariner".

This letter is dated 18 December 1497, by which time Cabot had already made his first voyage. In scarcely more than two years, he, "a foreigner and a poor man", had obtained an audience with the king, had been granted letters patent, had equipped and crewed a ship, and had "gained a part of Asia [as it was believed to be] without a stroke of the sword". Although it is only to the point as expressing the usually unhurried nature of the age, it is impossible to omit the last sentence of the ambassador's letter: "Meanwhile I stay on in this country, eating ten or twelve courses at each meal, and spending three hours at table twice a day, for love of Your Excellency."

Whether or not it was done over working dinners Cabot's business arrangements were completed with such celerity that we must go back to sift the details—and come on the first snags.

The letters patent were dated 5 March 1496. They granted "to our welbeloved

John Cabot citizen of Venice, to Lewis, Sebastian and Santius, sonnes of the sayd John ... leave and power to saile to all parts, contreys, and seas of the East, of the West, and of the North". It was as free and generous a mandate as could be given. Cabot and his sons were granted freedom from all customs duty on such trade goods as they might bring back, though the king reserved to himself 20 per cent "of the capitale gaine so gotten".

Armed with the letters patent Cabot returned to Bristol to organize the expedition. He had been allowed five ships, but he appears to have taken only one, the *Mathew*, a vessel of about fifty tons and needing a crew of not more than twenty. Even so small a number of trustworthy volunteers were difficult to find in Cabot's pioneering days.

Fear of physical discomfort is unlikely to have discouraged crews from signing on. The standard of comfort on ships of that period was low in any case and conditions below decks can scarcely have been worse than the conditions in which the poor lived at the time. Fear of the unknown was the real deterrent. Nobody knew what to expect, what hazards might be met, whether anything at all would be found.

Also, for whatever reason, sailors tend to be superstitious. Centuries ago they were no doubt more so, and with less tradition behind them they made up their omens as they went along. Coleridge's *Ancient Mariner* poetically expresses this. While the weather was favourable the shooting of the albatross augured well, but when things went badly the killing was the cause. As an actual instance, the variation of the compass as Columbus's *Santa Maria* crossed the meridians was a major cause of anxiety. Even if America had not existed, Columbus would not have reached the coast of Asia. Mutiny came too near during the thirty-six days of sailing between the Canary Islands and the Bahamas.

Mutinies bedevilled early exploration, and it was not unknown for ships simply to desert the fleet with which they were sailing and turn home. These mutinies were seldom violent, and in only a few instances did they cause loss of life. The word "strikes" might describe them better, but not fully: strikes can be settled by more pay, but sailors who have reached the point when they believe themselves doomed to die if they go any further are not open to any inducement to continue. Offer a fortune to a man condemned to be hanged and it does not alter the subject of his concentration. Therefore, to avoid the growth of that pessimism that leads to mutiny, voyages out of sight of land had to be as short as possible.

This brings us to the essential difference between Cabot's plan and Columbus's. The circumference of the earth is very much less in the latitude of England than it is in the latitude of the Canary Islands. Therefore a voyage of equal length to Columbus's would take Cabot, on the route he had chosen, much further round the world. (The cosmographers later calculated that a north-western route to the East would save some 6,000 miles.) Cabot thus expected that he would make his landfall to the north of the rich districts described by Marco Polo, after which he would be at leisure to explore further south.

Bristol was the best place to organize such a voyage. As a port it was second only to London, and its seamen were the most enterprising in the country. Since at least 1480 they had been looking for islands called the Seven Cities and for an Isle of Brasil (nothing to do with what we now know as Brazil) in the ocean to the west. They did not associate these with Cathay, but sought new bases for their fishermen—for there were already international difficulties about Icelandic fishing. Cabot had to convert this real yet limited enterprise into enthusiasm for finding a trade route to Cathay. It took him about a year, but he succeeded. He convinced merchants and seamen of the validity of a plan that would cut out the upstart rival Southampton, the little port to which Venetian ships brought oriental goods for England.

In May 1497 the *Mathew* sailed from Bristol on a westerly course, and after a passage of thirty-five days (one less than Columbus had taken in sailing from the Canary Islands to the Bahamas) reached an island, off Cape Breton, Nova Scotia, that Cabot named St John. The naming of Prima Terra Vista is also mentioned in the accounts, and is naturally associated with Newfoundland.

Cabot landed on forested coast. He saw no one, but there were signs of human activity: a burnt-out fire, a track, some felled trees, snares and a netting needle. It was St John's day, 24 June, sunny and hot. One can imagine the shadows cast by the trees, the silence, and the anxious speculation on what the forest hid. The handful of Bristol men and the Venetian raised the banners of England and of Venice, filled their water casks and returned to their ship. One wonders what the natives made of the flags.

That was the only landing during the voyage. The explorers spent the next month following the coastline east and south and covered 900 miles, but never ventured far-enough inshore to be certain how much was inhabited. They then turned for home and made a remarkably rapid, if somewhat inaccurate, passage, sighting Brittany within a fortnight and reaching Bristol by 6 August.

John Cabot left no record of his voyages himself (indeed, we have not one word written by him), and there is no proof that his son Sebastian, was aboard the *Mathew*. The second-hand records we possess are more vague than this summary suggests, and in parts are contradictory. But Cabot had done, or believed he had done, what he had set out to do on this first reconnaissance. He could not, with a single small ship, have planned to trade. He had found the shortest route to the land across the ocean and had followed the coast far enough to ensure that it was not merely a chain of islands. Trade would follow as a matter of course. No one in 1497 suspected the existence of another continent. Therefore Cabot had reached the mainland of Cathay, without obstacle or difficulty.

The English king had every reason to be delighted. (Henry had never admitted the validity of the Treaty of Tordesillas, which had divided between Spain and Portugal all the lands that remained to be discovered.) He promptly granted Cabot a pension of £20 and fresh letters patent. These were similar to those of two years earlier, but omitted mention of Cabot's sons and stated that he could take as crew "such masters, mariners, and subjects of the king as willingly go with him".

For this second voyage Cabot had no trouble in finding volunteers. Enthusiasm was high. An Italian wrote of the explorer, "Vast honour is paid him; he dresses in silk, and these English run after him like mad people."

Five ships took part in the voyage of 1498: one provided by the king and the rest by the merchants of London and Bristol. They sailed from Bristol in May. Soon after reaching open sea, one vessel suffered damage and put into an Irish port for repair. That is all we know for certain.

It may reasonably be assumed that the voyage was planned to develop the reconnaissance of 1497. This rules out any likelihood that Cabot aimed further north; for he believed he had found Cathay, and was now looking for the rich areas further south. With five ships and stores for a year, he would search the coast more thoroughly than before.

But it cannot be supposed that the little fleet kept together. In storm or fog the vessels were likely to be separated, and, with no possibility of fixing an accurate rendezvous, they would be unlikely to come together again. It is of interest to note that, in his instructions for the first North-East Passage voyage, half a century later, Sebastian Cabot stressed the necessity of keeping in touch.

We have no record that any of the five ships in the 1498 expedition returned to England, but this does not mean that none survived. Probably one or two of them straggled home—with nothing much to report—after hope had been abandoned and public interest lost. Indeed, it is possible that Sebastian took part in the voyage, reached home, and said nothing.

What happened to John Cabot? It has been assumed that he returned to England, because there is a record of his pension of £20 having been paid between Christmas 1498 and Christmas 1499. But it is not recorded to whom it was paid. It might have been to his widow before his death could be legally assumed.

If Cabot succeeded in exploring further, he would no doubt have realized that the land he had found was not part of Asia, but an extension of the obstacle that Columbus had encountered. Had he then returned to England, there would surely be some record of the disappointment that his news brought to the merchants and officials who had backed him. Columbus, internationally praised for his voyage, was no less well documented during the period of his disgrace. Indeed, disgrace following upon success is perhaps of even greater news value than success itself.

But there is not a word about what happened to John Cabot. This suggests that memory of the expedition gradually faded, as time went by and nothing definite was heard. Cabot's return, whatever the news he brought, would have stimulated some sort of reaction, whether of praise, sympathy or criticism.

Interestingly, however, it seems from the La Cosa map of 1500 that at about this time an English ship's company charted a stretch of the isthmus of Panama near to where the canal has since been cut. Although we know of no alternative, we cannot presume that it was one of Cabot's ships that did this, still less that it was the vessel that he commanded. But it is nevertheless a possibility.

John Cabot is a sympathetic character, and he is important in our history as the leader of the first English trans-oceanic voyage. Burial at sea by the hand of man or nature is the most anonymous end that anyone can have; but one feels that he would have preferred it to returning with the admission that he had been wrong.

Chapter 4

Sebastian Cabot's Secret

After the first Spanish voyages to the west and the Portuguese discovery of the southern tip of Africa, the pope (Alexander VI) had been quick to see the danger of rivalry between the two great Catholic powers of the Iberian Peninsula. In a judgement similar to Solomon's, he divided the possible prize in two, decreeing that all lands west of a line 370 leagues west of the Cape Verde Islands should be open to exploration and exploitation by Spain, and that Portugal should have a monopoly of new lands discovered east of this line. The line ran safely to the European side of the West Indies, but cut off the shoulder of still-undiscovered South America—which is why Brazil speaks Portuguese. Spain and Portugal approved the papal ruling by signing the Treaty of Tordesillas in 1494; and the treaty was observed long enough for the pattern of Spanish and Portuguese expansion to be set.

By 1550 Portugal was established in India, had gained control of the trade routes to the Spice Islands further east, and had reached China and Japan. This little country, which on a globe can be covered by a finger tip, had captured the fabulous commerce of the Orient. It had even probed north-westward beyond Newfoundland, notably under Gaspar Corte Real. But the ships of both Gaspar and his brother Miguel, who went to look for him, were lost with all hands. We can take it that neither of them reached further north than the stony coast of Labrador.

By 1550 the Spaniards had conquered the Aztec and Inca empires and their galleons were rolling homeward laden with treasure. Magellan, a Portuguese leading a Spanish fleet, had discovered the straits bearing his name and had crossed the terrifyingly broad Pacific, one of his ships continuing, after his death in the Philippines, to make the first circumnavigation of the globe.

England, meanwhile, had done nothing in the field of exploration—unless Sebastian Cabot had reached the threshold of the North-West Passage. Whether he did or not is a matter of some doubt, and has to be deduced from claims, probabilities and possibilities.

A prime point to be decided is when Sebastian Cabot could have made such a voyage. He appears to have lived and worked in Bristol until 1512, after which he transferred his allegiance to Spain, where he became pilot major. He held this important post until 1548, when he returned to England to organize an expedition to the north-east. He remained on English soil until his death in 1557.

His youthfulness apart, there is good reason for believing that Sebastian could not have led a voyage to the north-west before 1505. His father's voyages had taken place in 1497 and 1498, and during the first few years of the sixteenth century exploratory voyages to the north-west—but getting no further than fishing banks—were made by a Bristol syndicate. We have the names of the men principally involved and Cabot is not among them. He first appears in the records in 1505, as having been awarded a pension of £10 by Henry VII for "diligent service"—a small recompense, probably for work in cartography and the study of navigation.

We have thus established the period 1505–12 as available for the voyage in question.

Now let us consider a statement made by Sebastian himself while pilot major of Spain. The statement is included in the second volume of the *Navigations* of Battista Ramusio, an acquaintance of Sebastian's, and is here given in contemporary translation:

When my father departed from Venice many years since to dwell in England, to follow the trade of merchandises, hee took mee with him to the Citie of London, while I was very young, yet having neverthelesse some knowledge of letters of humanitie, and of the sphere. And when my father died in that time when newes were brought that Don Christopher Colonus Genuese had discovered the coasts of India, whereof was great talke in all the Court of king Henry the 7, who then raigned, insomuch that all men with great admiration affirmed it to be a thing more divine then humane, to saile by the West into the

East where spices growe, by a way that was never knowen before, by this fame
and report there increased in my heart a great flame of desire to attempt some
notable thing. And understanding by reason of the Sphere, that if I should saile
by way of the North-west, I should by a shorter tract come into India, I
thereupon caused the King to be advertised of my devise, who immediatly
commanded two Carvels to bee furnished with all things appertayning to the
voyage, which was as farre as I remember in the yeere 1496, in the beginning of
Sommer. I began therefore to saile toward the North-west, not thinking to
finde any other land then that of Cathay, & from thence to turne toward India,
but after certain dayes I found that the land ranne towards the North, which
was to mee a great displeasure. Neverthelesse, sayling along by the coast to see
if I could finde any gulfe that turned, I found the lande still continent to the 56.
degree under our Pole. And seeing that there the coast turned toward the East,
despairing to finde the passage, I turned back againe, and sailed downe by the
coast of that land toward the Equinoctiall (ever with intent to finde the saide
passage to India) and came to that part of this firme lande which is nowe called
Florida, where my victuals failing, I departed from thence and returned into
England, where I found great tumults among the people, and preparation for
warres in Scotland: by reason whereof there was no more consideration had to
this voyage.

One's first reaction is to repeat, what happened to John Cabot? Apparently he
came to England only to die while his second son, a very young man, gained royal
patronage and led an expedition of two ships that explored as far north as latitude
56°, near the northern point of Labrador, and as far south as Florida—virtually
the whole Atlantic coast of North America. The date he gives, 1496, is when
letters patent were granted to his father, himself and his two brothers. His return
to "great tumults" seems to suggest the Scottish troubles and Perkin Warbeck's
attempt on the throne, in 1497.

A most unsatisfactory witness if not a downright liar, one feels. While in Spain
he gave other versions of the story, but there is no record that he gave any account
of it before leaving England.

Peter Martyr, an Italian living in Spain, was a personal friend of
Sebastian's—the only one of whom we know. He briefly records in his *De Orbe
Novo Decades* (no mean work) that Sebastian led to the north-west an expedition
of two ships and 300 men, organized at his own expense. Even supposing that
Sebastian had the money (which would have been much more than any individual,
the king included, had ever paid out for an expedition of this sort), it is incredible
that he should have wanted 300 men and the big, deep-draught ships necessary to
carry them.

Yet Martyr believed him at first hand, and the story was accepted by other sixteenth-century historians—the Spaniard Francisco Lopez de Gomara, the Frenchman André Thevet, Antonio Galvão of Portugal, and the Englishman Richard Willes. Furthermore, many of the great men of the century—Henry VII, Henry VIII, Cardinal Wolsey, the Venetian Senate, Ferdinand V of Castile, and the Holy Roman Emperor Charles V (Charles I of Spain)—believed Sebastian.

During his long service in Spain Cabot enjoyed the full confidence of his royal masters. Between 1526 and 1530 he commanded an expedition that tried to establish a colony on the Rio de la Plata; and, though on his return he was heavily fined, and condemned to serve four years in the penal colony in Morocco (having proved himself thoroughly unpopular, and an unsuccessful leader), Charles, returning from abroad, reprieved him and reinstated him as pilot major of Spain. Sebastian was always at his best with kings.

Ten years earlier Charles had allowed him to pay a long visit to England at the invitation of Henry VIII. This was done officially, as Cabot remained in the service of Spain, but it is most unlikely that Charles knew the real reason for the visit. Henry VIII, who previously had shown little or no interest in exploration, wanted expert advice about a projected voyage to the north-west. He and his shrewd Cardinal must have believed that Sebastian had something of real value to offer.

The idea came to nothing, but Cabot, perhaps as a result of his disappointment, talked with less discretion than usual to Venetian merchants in London. They were interested, but were not themselves able to sponsor a voyage.

On returning to his duties in Spain, Cabot began flirting with the idea of a visit to Venice and started a correspondence about an ancient inheritance that he believed was due to him and that he would have to visit Venice to collect. This seems to have been little more than a cover for his real interests.

He was shocked when the Venetian ambassador personally handed to him a letter from the Senate inviting him to come to Venice and expound his project. What had started in private conversations in London was being considered at the highest level, and might well reach the ears of the king of Spain himself.

The Venetian ambassador's report of this incident is long and specific. Sebastian Cabot turned pale and said, "I most earnestly beseech you to keep the thing secret, or it would cost me my life."

There is nothing like fear for bringing out the truth, or what the person concerned believes to be the truth. Sebastian Cabot believed that he had found the North-West Passage to Cathay, and was trying to play safe until he could sell this tremendously valuable secret. But a voyage, involving mariners and backers, cannot be kept entirely secret, even if the commander does not disclose geographical details. The Venetian Senate made their own inquiries.

In the report prepared for them it was stated that on his return to England from the voyage in question Sebastian Cabot found "the King dead and his son cared little for such an enterprise". This means that Cabot started his voyage during the reign of Henry VII and ended it after his death in April 1509. That Henry VIII was not, at first, particularly interested in exploration explains why Sebastian transferred to Spain three years later.

He had found a good new job, the best for which any navigator could hope; but a merchant with a monopoly to offer might make much more. He could not sell his secret in Spain. Spain was already fully committed in America, drinking in so much treasure that the galleons floated below the safety line; she would not be interested in an alternative to Magellan's route to the Pacific. Yet she would intensely resent it if another country found such an alternative.

Therefore not only could Sebastian Cabot not sell his secret to Spain, he had for his life to keep secret that he had offered it to another country. That is why he talked nothing but lies and vagaries while he was employed by Spain. But, when he was back in England for good, he felt safe in giving the information that Ramusio reports in the preface to the third volume of his *Discoveries* (1548).

"He advertised mee, that having sailed a long time West and by North, beyond those ilands unto the Latitude of 67 degrees and an halfe, under the North Pole, and at the 11 day of June finding still the open Sea without any manner of impediment, he thought verily by that way to have passed on still the way to Cathaia, which is in the East, and would have done it, if the mutinie of the shipmaster and Mariners had not hindered him and made him returne homewards from that place. But it seemeth that God doeth still reserve this great enterprise for some great prince to discover this voyage to Cathaia by this way, which for the bringing of the spiceries from India into Europe, were the most easie and shortest of all other wayes hitherto found out."

The first part of this—specifying the date and latitude and mentioning the freedom from ice and the outbreak of mutiny (an experience that later explorers would have in what was probably the same area)—is much more circumstantial than Ramusio's earlier account. The latter part is a hook baited for a royal patron. There is still no description of how to reach the passage; the secret remained to be bought.

Ramusio also gives a description of the American coastline south of where the mutiny occurred, and mentions that the vast quantity of fish in the sea sometimes delayed the ships. Cabot named the land Baccalaos, which, with slight variations in spelling, is the word still used in Mediterranean countries for dried and salted cod.

An exploration of the seaboard between latitudes 67° and 40° would have taken more than a season, and thus would have meant wintering in a strange continent—a considerable adventure. This makes the report that there were 300 men in the expedition quite fantastic, and suggests instead that the company would have been small and carefully selected, and the ships (or ship) likewise. On balance, the accounts of Cabot's voyage that date from *after* his return from Spain can be considered credible. The most probable date for the voyage is 1508–9.

So far we have not considered the evidence provided by maps. In 1577 Richard Willes wrote of a map drawn by Sebastian himself; this has been lost, but Willes's description of the latitude, breadth, direction and length of the strait that Sebastian took to be the North-West Passage fits, with a striking degree of accuracy, what we now call Hudson Strait. It opened southward into the Pacific, Willes said; in fact it opens southward into the huge Hudson Bay, but the mistake is understandable.

Although Sebastian's map is lost, there remains one copy of a globe that our knowledge of the date of his voyage makes useful—the globe of Gemma Frisius, said to date from 1537. This depicts in the right place, in its entirety and opening into an "ocean" a strait similar to that described above. No map or globe dating from before 1509 does that. On the southern shore is a note: "Terra per britannos inventa" ("Land discovered by Britons"). Gemma Frisius calls the strait the Strait of the Three Brothers, which suggests the brothers Cabot: Sebastian, Ludovico and Sancio (it would be typical of Sebastian not to mention his brothers' participation).

We have no firm proof that Sebastian Cabot reached Hudson Strait, but it is in no way impossible that he did so, even if his ship was much smaller than he claimed. There is too much written about the "cockleshells" of the early explorers; they were stout little hearts of oak. The North-West Passage was finally navigated, four centuries later, in a herring-boat of forty-seven tons. Why should the first voyage not have been made in a fishing craft similar to those already sailing to Iceland and Newfoundland, if not beyond? And that would make it understandable why the venture was not officially recorded.

As a man Sebastian is difficult to like: untruthful, unfilial, egocentric. But because he kept his discovery to himself he cannot justly be called unpatriotic, for he belonged completely to no country. He was one of the corps of mercenary navigators who did more for early exploration than did any devoted patriot.

Chapter 5

Experiment in the North-East

Sebastian Cabot never managed to sell his secret, but he got a good price for the reputation he had built up. In 1547 Edward VI (or rather his regents, for the king was a child) offered him an "annuitie or yerely revenue" of £166 13s 4d—a good salary in those days, particularly for a man of about sixty-five. Cabot accepted and left Spain so promptly that he may almost be said to have run away. By this time he had kept his secret too long to act on it himself, even with the best backing in the world, and the wind of interest had swung to another quarter. He was enough of a sailor, or psychologist, to trim his sails accordingly.

He became governor of the "Mysterie and Companie of the Merchant Adventurers for the Discoverie of Regions, Dominions and Places Unknown", whose first aim was to reach the Orient by sailing north-east, but whose operations were not restricted to any particular area. The establishment of the company is historically important, since it set the financial pattern of such ventures for the next two centuries. Because of this, and owing to the light it sheds on what motivated these ventures, it is necessary to give here some account of the company and the first voyage it organized.

The word "Mysterie" in the company's name signifies a trading concern: the object of the enterprise was trade. The "Adventurers" were investors: shares of £25 each were publicly offered, and in this way capital of £6,000 was soon available and three ships bought. (This trading by a company, now obvious enough, had evolved from the medieval guild system, the guild being something like a co-operative. Different producers and processes had to be co-ordinated, so a middleman of no particular allegiance was needed as organizer. He, in modern terms, was the chairman or managing director.) The Adventurers, who provided the capital, might live anywhere and follow any profession—though most would have described themselves as gentlemen. The personal adventure of each might double or disappear on the other side of the world, but the chances were clearly better if the company was well directed. That is where Cabot came in: his knowledge, experience and reputation were considered essential to raise the capital and launch the ships.

As governor, Cabot was in charge of preparations for the voyage, started six years after his appointment, in search of the North-East Passage. One of his responsibilities would have been to set the course to be sailed, but neither he nor anybody else could have said more than that the North Cape had to be rounded and the coast of Lapland passed. No doubt he chose the ships: *Edward Bonaventure* (160 tons), *Bona Esperanza* (120 tons) and *Bona Confidentia* (ninety tons)—names that are optimistic, but ("Edward" apart) un-English. Foreign and optimistic too was the manner in which the ships were specially prepared: their hulls were sheathed in lead to protect them against the sea worms of the tropics.

We may suppose that English merchants handled the cargo. They must have trusted themselves that far; and, besides, there was no choice: the best broadcloth in the world, for Calais or Cathay.

As for discipline at sea, we have "Ordinances, instructions, and advertisements for the direction of the intended voyage for Cathay, compiled, made and delivered by the right worshipfull M. Sebastian Cabota Esquier . . . in the yere of our Lord God 1553." In effect these are the first standing orders for an expedition that must pass through arctic waters. It is interesting to consider them in the light of what we know of the character and experience of the former pilot major of Spain.

There are thirty-three items. The first few are naive exhortations; the rest social, moral, political (democratically so) and commercial, rather than nautical. It is the headmaster's address to the boys at the opening of a new school.

Everyone, from captain-general to mariner, is required to swear on oath to do his best, the only differentiation being that more is expected of the officers, merchants, "and other skilful persons". A full and scientific record of the voyage is to be maintained, and records and accounts are to be kept of all the food and drink consumed, equipment, earnings (including what is due to the next of kin of anyone who dies), and so on and so forth. It is all very scrupulous. Mariners may wear their "liveries in apparel" only on special occasions and at the captain's orders. Their "necessarie furniture" is accounted for, and concern is shown for their health. The sick must be cared for and their place of duty be taken by another without question. For reasons of hygiene, "No liquor to be split on the balast, nor filthiness to be left within boord: the cook room, and all other places to be kept cleane for the better health of the companie."

Stress is laid on consultation. The captain-general is in charge, but the pilot major, mates and "counsailers" (probably merchants) may have their say. The fleet is to keep together, and the officers, petty officers and "counsailers" must be ready to go aboard the Admiral (the leading vessel) for discussion.

There must be "no blaspheming of God, or detestable swearing ... ribaldrie, filthy tales ... dicing, carding, tabling, nor other divelish games." Prayers are to be said night and morning, but the religion of any country visited is to be respected without comment. That did not come from Spain!

On the other hand, "There are people that can swimme in the sea, havens and rivers, naked, having bowes and shafts ... desirous of the bodies of men, which they covet for meate", but, "If you shall see they weare Lyons or Beares skinnes, having long bowes and arrowes, be not afraid of that sight: for such be worne oftentimes to feare strangers." Here is a whiff of service in South America.

There are strict rules against tampering with the cargo in any way. There is strong emphasis on the necessity for good and non-aggressive behaviour in foreign lands. All are to behave as English ambassadors, and there is to be a "modest and temperate dispending of powder and shot and use of all kinds of artillery, which is not to be misused, but diligently to be preserved for the necessary defense of the fleets and voyage."

The sailors are encouraged to bring aboard people from foreign lands, to give them wine and learn all they can from them, but "without violence or force, and no woman to be tempted or intreated to incontinencie or dishonestie". Even under provocation "faire words" are to be given.

This point is stressed in a letter signed by Edward VI (then aged fifteen), translated into several languages, including Greek, and addressed to the rulers of such countries as should be visited. It asks that the voyagers should be treated humanely. "They shall not touch anything of yours unwilling unto you."

Is this the king's own voice speaking? Cabot, who did not sail on the voyage and seems to have been involved in it purely in an administrative capacity, appears to have been little more than a figurehead as governor. By contrast, no Tudor (not even the young Edward) was ever a mere figurehead. To what extent did the king supervise Sebastian Cabot's Ordinances? It is an evocative picture: an ailing young monarch, passionately religious and patriotic, working with a tough old navigator of no national allegiance at the document that raised the curtain on English exploration of the North.

The voyage, as it turned out, provided an object lesson in what could go wrong in the Arctic in spite of careful preparations, and what might, quite unexpectedly, prove profitable.

The three ships, commanded by Sir Hugh Willoughby (captain-general of the fleet), Richard Chancellor and Cornelius Durforth, were towed down the Thames on 11 May 1553. To mark the occasion, the mariners were dressed in their sky-blue liveries. Richard Eden described the scene as the ships passed Greenwich Palace: "The courtiers came running out, and the common people flockt together, standing very thicke upon the shoare: the privie Counsel, they lookt out of the windowes of the Court, and the rest ranne up to the toppes of the towers: the shippes hereupon discharge their Ordance, and shoot off their pieces. . . . But (alas) the good King Edward (in respect of whom principally all this was prepared) hee only by reason of his sicknesse was absent from the shewe."

The ships had been provisioned for eighteen months. At Harwich it was discovered that some of the victuals were "curupt and putrified" and that the hogsheads of wine were leaking. Much worse was to follow. The little fleet was dispersed by a storm. Only Chancellor's *Edward Bonaventure* reached the White Sea in the autumn.

Chancellor led a party overland to Moscow—a journey of 1,500 miles. They were much impressed by the vast and thickly forested country ("Rich and poore at time of death assured of coffins stand"!) and were welcomed with warmth and curiosity by Ivan the Terrible. He entertained them at his table and took in his hand an English beard "five foote and two inches of assize".

The closest that the *Edward Bonaventure* got to Cathay was Archangel, but her voyage opened trade with Russia, a mutually valuable commerce that grew rapidly. It is at a send-off party for Stephen Borough, Chancellor's shipmaster, on a subsequent voyage to Russia that we have our last glimpse of Sebastian Cabot. He treated the ship's company at a Gravesend tavern and himself joined in the dancing with "the young and lusty company". In his last years he became a "good old gentleman" who still dreamed his dreams but no longer schemed his schemes.

As for the *Bona Esperanza* and *Bona Confidentia*, their fate was discovered when a search ship found their lead-sheathed hulls and sixty-six bodies on a barren stretch of the east Lapland coast.

What killed them? They had not drowned. Presumably the ships had grounded or been caught by ice. But, even if damaged beyond repair, each carried a pinnace and a boat, which might have been used the following summer. So it was the winter that killed them; but why? Their victuals would surely have lasted at least a year (the loss mentioned had been on the *Edward Bonaventure*), and, although the coast was uninhabited, hunting might have added something. Driftwood was available to supplement fuel; the men had plenty of clothing and a cargo of broadcloth.

Perhaps they simply died of fear and despair. If so, this was not caused by anything approaching complete darkness. They were not far north of the Arctic Circle and the sun would have stayed below the horizon for only two or three weeks at most. In clear weather the sky of the Arctic night is brilliant, and at mid-day there would have been at least a dawn glow.

It is possible that some of the crew were snuffed out by carbon-monoxide poisoning. If men seal themselves off in a cabin and stoke up the stove, the odourless and invisible gas collects, and kills as suddenly as a bullet in the brain. The description given in a letter written by the Venetian ambassador to England would be consistent with such an accident: "The mariners now returned from the second voyage narrate strange things about the mode in which they [the victims from the two ships] were frozen, having found some of them seated in the act of writing, pen in hand, and the paper before them, others at table, platter in hand and spoon in mouth; others opening a locker, and others in various postures, like statues, as if they had been adjusted and placed in those attitudes."

The bodies would, of course, be frozen after death. However, carbon-monoxide poisoning cannot account for all the victims, for they would not have been all together at once. Doubtless such an accident occurred, and weakened the resistance of the survivors.

We lack the data to make it worth inquiring further, which would not be appropriate here. What matters is that this tragedy increased existing fear of the arctic night. It was many years before a voyage was made with the *intention* of wintering in the north; each expedition played tip and run, seeking to keep half the short summer season for getting out of the ice and home again. When wintering was at last accepted, exploring time was doubled or more; but it was a severe test for the commander, who had to keep his men sound in mind and body during the long months of inactivity.

Chapter 6

Frobisher and the North-West Bubble

The success-*cum*-tragedy of the 1553 expedition must not be overstressed from
the national point of view. One attempt was made to push further north-
eastward, but ended undramatically. There was no surge of interest in northern
exploration—quite the reverse. Even Newfoundland, that magic word, meant an
international fishing ground, where, fortunately, there was enough fruit of the sea
for English, French, Spanish and Portuguese to reap their harvests without
serious incident. It was the cod banks that mattered; nobody bothered to map the
land. The French, led by Jacques Cartier, were planting their roots in the seed-bed
of the St Lawrence, even though it had proved not to be the North-West Passage;
but until the next century few in England saw further than the banks. One hopes
that John Donne's mistress was out of the ordinary, or when he exclaimed, "Oh,
my America! My new-found-land!" she might have thought he was suggesting
that she smelt of fish.

Of course, there were extraordinary individuals during the latter half of the
sixteenth century—at least as many as in any other fifty-year period; but there
were very few whose prime interest was geographical, or even commercial or
colonial, exploration. Queen Mary, apart from her hot religious activity, was

largely preoccupied with the loss of Calais. That finally made Englishmen look outwards from the continent. Queen Elizabeth's sailors were encouraged to range far and wide. They realized the vastness of the ocean and its potential. Yet Drake wanted no inch of Spanish soil, and Raleigh was not a successful colonizer. Privateering rather than the navy or mercantile marine was the school of seamanship, and its playing field was the southern ocean.

A few longsighted men looked to the arctic seas, but before we come to them we must make a point of the greatest importance. It has often been said that England sailed north-westward because Spain and Portugal dominated the southern seas and the north-east had proved impracticable; in other words, because it was her last chance of finding a route to Cathay. That is wrong. By the time England lashed her helm, Portugal was in decline and Spain was no longer feared. We shall be talking later of two men who explored before the Armada. But in their hearts it had already been defeated. They were looking for the best and shortest route to the East, not a back way by which powerful rivals might be avoided. The round trip to the Orient by way of the Cape of Good Hope took a couple of years; the Straits of Magellan were useful for communication with the western American seaboard but not for Cathay, because of the immense span of the Pacific. That was the argument for finding a short-cut over the top of the world. Meanwhile Elizabethan sailors went where they pleased as far as human enemies were concerned. They accepted the risks involved, welcomed them even.

In 1589, the year after the Armada, Richard Hakluyt wrote as follows in the dedication of his *Voyages*:

To speak a word of that just commendation which our nation doe indeed deserve: it can not be denied, but as in all former ages, they have bene men full of activity, stirrers abroad, and searchers of the remote parts of the world, so in this most famous and peerlesse governement of her most excellent Majesty, her subjects through the speciall assistance, and blessing of God, in searching the most opposite corners and quarters of the world, and to speake plainly, in compassing the vaste globe of the earth more then once, have excelled all the nations and people of the earth. For, which of the kings of this land before her Majesty, had theyr banners ever seene in the Caspian sea? which of them hath ever dealt with the Emperor of Persia, as her Majesty hath done, and obtained for her merchants large & loving privileges? who ever saw before this regiment, an English Ligier in the stately porch of the Grand Signor at Constantinople? who ever found English Consuls & Agents at Tripolis in Syria, at Aleppo, at Babylon, at Balsara, and which is more, who ever heard of Englishmen at Goa before now? what English shippes did heeretofore ever anker in the mighty river of Plate? passe and repasse the unpassable (in former opinion) straight of Magellan, range along the coast of Chili, Peru, and all the backside of Nova Hispania, further then any Christian ever passed, travers the mighty bredth of the South sea, land upon the Luzones in despight of the enemy, enter into alliance, amity, and traffike with the princes of the Moluccaes, & the Isle of Java, double the famous Cape of Bona Speranza, arrive at the Isle of Santa Helena, & last of al returne home most richly laden with the commodities of China, as the subjects of this now florishing monarchy have done?

Sebastian Cabot, of course, had searched for the North-West Passage as the best and shortest way; but his heart was bound to no country and his motive had been to make his own fortune. The Elizabethan motive was different. Although not altruistic (there was always the chance of making a fortune), it was basically patriotic, with death or glory as the spur. It was like putting up an idea for a commando raid and asking to be included. Since in this case security was not involved, there was no attempt at secrecy; quite the reverse. The idea was to be publicized, promoted.

Consider Sir Humphrey Gilbert. An aristocrat, a courtier, a Member of Parliament, a kinsman of Raleigh, a scholar of Eton and Oxford, a soldier, he was anything but a merchant. He was a geographer of infinite research; enough of a poet and philosopher to exclaim in a storm, "We are as near to heaven by sea as by land", a pioneer who planted a colony on Newfoundland and who lost his life before he was forty-five because he insisted on sailing in the smallest ship of his fleet, which overturned.

Here we are concerned only with his *Discourse on a North West Passage to India*, which he composed in 1566 and published with a map ten years later. In the first chapter he states that "any man of our country, that will give the attempt may with small danger passe to Cataia, the Moluccae, India, and all other places of the East, in much shorter time, then either the Spaniard, or Portugal doeth, or may doe".

Later in his *Discourse* he quotes Pliny, Cornelius Nepos, Frederick Barbarossa and Gemma Frisius to prove that the passage by "the Straits of Anian" had already been used by Indians in the distant past and rediscovered by more modern man. But his map offers the clearest evidence: the passage to the Pacific is funnel-shaped and (as well as one can judge) several degrees of latitude in width at its narrowest point. The propaganda is as evident as in a poster. Certainly a pilot could not navigate by this; but Gilbert states, "Sebastian Cabota . . . set foorth and described this passage in his Charts, which are yet to be seene in the Queens Majesties privie Gallerie at Whitehall." Therefore they were available to anyone contemplating a voyage at that time.

Part of Gilbert's military service was spent in savage and useless attempts to discipline the wild Irish. In that country in about 1570 he met Martin Frobisher, who was then similarly employed by the Queen. The two men were of the same age but very different in background and education. Frobisher was a Yorkshire yeoman and on his mother's side had connections with the gentry. As for education, he was at sea by the age of fifteen. It was a tough school. In the same year as Willoughby and Chancellor sailed north-east, Frobisher served as a boy on one of the three ships taken by Thomas Wyndham to the Guinea coast for gold and pepper. The Portuguese considered these waters their monopoly and opposed interlopers. But fever and shipwreck were greater dangers. From this voyage only forty of the original 140 returned to England. Disease came not only from the fevered land but was bred in the close and insanitary conditions on board. With the manifold perils of a reckless trade, a mariner's expectation of life was short.

Frobisher probably engaged in slave-gathering and certainly in piracy. The Spanish ambassador protested to the Privy Council that Frobisher had plundered a ship from Andalusia, and he stood trial in the Admiralty Court for a similar offence against the Flemish subjects of King Philip. That such a man should not only remain free but be recruited by the Queen is explained by Elizabeth's policy of harrassing Spain without actually declaring war. Frobisher was an unusually rough example of a rough and ready age. His striking characteristics were courage, energy and ambition. He was of tremendous physical strength and very brittle temper.

Sir Humphrey Gilbert's military duty of cutting off Irish heads did not divert him from his geographical thesis—that Magellan's Strait was complemented by a similar, Arctic passage, the Straits of Anian. He talked to his strange friend about it, and Frobisher was enthusiastic. It is stated by George Best, his most literate chronicler (Frobisher himself wrote little more than his name, and spelt that in half a dozen different ways) that "he determined and resolved with himself to go make proofe there-of, or els never return againe, knowing this to be the only thing of the world that was left yet undone, whereby a noteable minde might be made famous and fortunate".

It was not, of course, the only thing. Drake, for instance, had not yet set out on his circumnavigation. Vast areas remained unexplored. But perhaps it was the only thing of which Frobisher, with little imagination and no scholarship, saw himself capable; and the passage to Cathay would bring fortune as well as fame. Even so, he needed patronage in high places. Gilbert helped him by bringing him to the notice of Commander-in-Chief Sir Henry Sidney, brother-in-law of the Earl of Warwick. Thus Frobisher's plan (to be more precise, the plan of the generous Gilbert, who longed to do the thing himself) reached the ears of Burghley, Walsingham, Leicester and Sir Philip Sidney.

Cathay meant riches. Riches meant gold. England was in urgent need of gold, for the country was suffering from inflation. If a source of wealth could be found as profitable and easy as that that Spain was exploiting in Mexico and Peru, the economy would be assisted without any need to alter the Queen's foreign policy. So the plan was approved in principle.

But financial backing had to be found and Frobisher was not the right person for this. The City distrusted a man with the reputation of a pirate, and the Muscovy Company openly opposed the voyage, because their charter gave them a monopoly to the north-west as well as the north-east. The Privy Council had to throw their weight if not their money onto the scale before £1,500 could be produced. This was finally achieved by the Muscovy Company's granting a licence for a subsidiary company, with Michael Lok, a director of the Muscovy, personally guaranteeing the whole amount. Some £8,600 had been subscribed by private investment, leaving a £7,000 loan to be covered. Lok, an experienced businessman, would scarcely have risked so much on the gamble of a short-cut route to Cathay, but he knew better than anyone what the Muscovy Company had incidentally gained by seeking the same destination. The north-western Arctic might produce furs, whale oil, or something else.

His money assured (the worst problem any explorer has to face) Frobisher bought, refitted and supplied the *Michael* and the *Gabriel* (of twenty-five and twenty tons respectively—small ocean ships by any standard). He was the General—a title given to leaders at sea as well as to leaders on land, the "Admiral" being the flagship, as noted earlier. Frobisher's shipmaster on the *Gabriel* was Christopher Hall, Owen Gryffyn being master of the *Michael*. The two crews together numbered thirty-two men and boys. They had no stake in the voyage. Their wage of a few shillings a week conveys little, the value of money being so much changed. A more useful gauge is that the daily ration of an Elizabethan sailor was one pound of bread, two pounds of salt beef and a gallon of beer. This might well have been an inducement in the state of high unemployment that then existed. Conditions had changed since the days of John Cabot.

The two little ships sailed from Blackwall on 7 June 1576. Opposite Greenwich Palace they fired a salute, less loud and impressive than that of Sir Hugh Willoughby's fleet twenty-three years earlier and with no crowd of well-wishers looking on. The Queen sent for the General and granted him a brief audience before he continued. She never showed for Frobisher, even in his later and more dramatic years, the affection she showed for Drake and Raleigh; but she allowed him to serve her, at the moment without any risk, financial or political.

Frobisher made three voyages to the Arctic, yet added little to geographical knowledge. His fame and knighthood were won later, in the long struggle against Spain that culminated in the defeat of the Armada, and he died from a wound received in battle. He had not the right temperament for an explorer, who needs the patience and ingenuity of defence rather than the impetuous courage of assault. But his comparative failure was chiefly owing to impetuosity of another sort, on the part of his backers. In tracing the chain of different motives that kept the search for the North-West Passage flowing, one finds no stretch more surprising than that covered by Frobisher's voyages. They show how rare a thing was reasoned thought in the fabulous new age of exploration.

One point that is particularly striking is that Frobisher depended on charts of very doubtful authenticity, nearly 200 years old. Although Sebastian Cabot's map was then available, he used the Zeno map.

The Zeno odyssey is bizarre. It is included in Hakluyt's *Voyages* and reads like a fairy story. In the year 1380 a rich Venetian named Nicolo Zeno had a ship built for himself, "as he was very wealthy", and sailed out of the Mediterranean to visit England and Flanders. But he was swept away by a storm and after many days wrecked on Frisland. After various adventures he met Prince Zichmni of Porland who gave him command of his navy of thirteen ships. Nicolo wrote to his brother Antonio (we are not told by what means) asking him to join him. Antonio did so, and together the brothers made many voyages for trade or conquest among the neighbouring countries of Estotiland, Engronland, Drogeo, Podalida, Neome, Islanda and Gronlandia. Several of these were most desirable countries where the people spoke Latin. After thirteen years the brothers returned to Venice.

The account of these voyages of 1380–93 was published in 1558. A descendant to Nicolo Zeno had transcribed it from letters he had found in a junk room of his house. There was also a map showing all these countries in the north Atlantic. The author stated, "I thought good to draw the copie of a sea carde, which among other antiquities I have in my house, which although it be rotten through many yeeres, yet it falleth out indifferent well." This sounds an appropriate beginning for a treasure hunt.

Besides the *Gabriel* and *Michael*, Frobisher had a pinnace with a crew of four, and each ship carried a boat. The little fleet rounded Scotland and headed north-west. On 11 July the bare black basalt mountains of east Greenland were sighted. Confused by his map, Frobisher called it Friesland.

Because of the heavy pack ice that continually drifts down that coast, he could not reach the shore, so he bore southward until he cleared the southern tip of Greenland. He suffered gales and fog, and lost contact with the other vessels. Owen Gryffyn took this opportunity to turn the *Michael* back to England. The pinnace foundered.

George Best, Frobisher's officer and chronicler, writes, "The worthy captaine [Frobisher in the *Gabriel*] notwithstanding these discomforts, although his mast was sprung, and his toppe mast blowen overboord with extreeme foule weather, continued his course towards the Northwest, knowing that the sea must needs have an ending, and that some land must have a beginning that way." Sure enough it did. On 20 July he sighted a mountain, which he called Queen's Foreland. To use modern nomenclature, he had reached Resolution Island, which lies off Baffin

Island and opposite Cape Chidley, the northernmost point of Labrador, with Hudson Strait opening between.

Beyond Resolution Island Frobisher entered a "gut" in south-east Baffin Island. It was narrow enough for him to see both shores, but according to Best he took it for granted that the land on the left was America and the land on the right Asia—in other words, that he had hit at once upon the North-West Passage after sailing blind through gale and fog.

This is not quite as credulous as it sounds, for the current geographical theory was that the extremity of Asia projected eastwards close above the American coast, and that the passage between opened out to the west. However, this took no account of Sebastian Cabot's description of a much wider passage, lying in much the same latitude as the "passage" that Frobisher had found. Frobisher called his discovery after himself, and the name is on modern maps—although as Frobisher Bay, not Frobisher Strait.

His plan was to push on until the channel opened into the Pacific. His method when the ice floes were numerous was to send the rowing boat ahead to nose out a passage and thus avoid the danger—ever present for a sailing vessel—of getting trapped. Thus he advanced for 180 miles. Then parties were sent ashore to gather Asiatic souvenirs.

The *Gabriel* was soon surrounded by kayaks. The Eskimos came aboard, were delighted to barter seal and bear skins for mirrors and little bells, and played about like children in the rigging. But disaster followed. Five of the *Gabriel's* crew rowed ashore and disappeared. It was presumed that they had been kidnapped.

Without the rowing boat Frobisher could not follow and search for them, and it would have been more difficult than before to continue the voyage. He decided to turn back. But before starting for home he managed to entice a kayaker close to the ship's side by tinkling a bell. When the native reached up for it, Frobisher leaned over the low gunwhale, caught his wrist and swung him aboard, kayak and all. With this "strange infidell" as a trophy he returned to England.

The Eskimo died of a cold soon after arrival. This is not surprising, for coming from the clinically clean Arctic air he could have had no resistance to a civilized complaint. He lived just long enough for his mongoloid features to be noted as proof that Asia had been reached.

But soon Cathay was forgotten in dreams of a still greater source of wealth. Frobisher gave to Michael Lok a dark-coloured stone that one of his mariners had picked up in Meta Incognita, as the land he had discovered was named by the scholarly queen. Lok, giving rein to his imagination, got it into his head that this stone, which was remarkable only for its weight, was rich in gold. He took it to the assay-master of the Tower, who told him that it was marcasite—iron pyrites. Unsatisfied, Lok had tests made by two professional metallurgists in the City. They independently declared that it was marcasite, which may contain minute traces of gold, but no more.

This was not good enough for Lok, and, having heard of an Italian assayer who was visiting London, he took it to him. This man found an appreciable proportion of gold.

That Lok was now satisfied is perhaps not surprising, for he had behaved throughout like the person who goes on asking advice until he is told what he wants to hear. But it *is* remarkable how quickly the story spread and how wildly it was exaggerated. Men of education and business, courtiers, the cream of Elizabethan society, believed that Frobisher had discovered priceless deposits of gold.

There was no difficulty in financing another voyage, or at any rate in obtaining the necessary credit. The Cathay Company was formed and the Queen herself bought a small share, thus providing royal patronage. The *Gabriel* and *Michael* were re-equipped and a 240-ton naval ship, the *Aid,* was lent to transport the ore. Michael Lok became governor of the new company.

Frobisher was High Admiral—a novel title. Just possibly he smiled, but there is no record of his ever having done so. His first voyage had been uncomfortable and inconclusive; without discovering that his "strait" was a cul-de-sac he had turned home, perhaps doubtful of his reception after his brave boast. Suddenly—and, we can be sure, quite unexpectedly to him—a stone that one of his mariners had touched had turned to gold. Hey, presto!—he was High Admiral.

His instructions were to lade the 200-tonner with ore, then continue his westward exploration in the *Gabriel* and *Michael.* Oddly, though, he made no attempt to sail further up his "strait", but confined himself to the search for gold-bearing ore. As no more iron pyrites could be found at the original site, he filled the holds of all three ships with promising rock from another part of Meta Incognita. All went smoothly, except on one occasion when the High Admiral and Christopher Hall, master of the *Aid,* went ashore unarmed to barter with the Eskimos. A quarrel developed, apparently because the Englishmen believed themselves to have been insulted. The natives became menacing, and, perhaps for the one and only time in his life, Frobisher ran away. He received an arrow in the buttock. He was not the sort of man to turn the other cheek. Later an armed party went ashore and killed five Eskimos.

Back in Bristol in October 1577, the 200 tons of mineral was unloaded and quickly stored away under strong guard. Gold dust or the dream of it had got into men's minds like yeast and transformed reason into a gambler's fantasies. The original souvenir, which must have been small, cannot have been analysed in more than marble-sized quantities, and then with only one favourable result out of four. Nothing more searching or thorough than laboratory experiments on small quantities was attempted with the 200 tons brought back on the second voyage. There was no smelting; the unproved fortune was locked away.

Michael Lok had trouble in paying off the crews. Many of the enthusiastic investors in the Cathay Company had so far neglected to pay for their shares, and the priceless mineral lay frozen in the vaults. There was no attempt to turn it into money. The Queen and everyone else concerned were as amiable and optimistic as could be, but there was a severe shortage of cash.

Within seven months Frobisher was sent off again, this time with no fewer than fifteen ships and with instructions demanding only the lading of ore. It was the biggest commercial gamble of the whole Tudor period, and the credit of the Cathay Company, under royal patronage, was stretched to the limit to cover it. Not even the most sagacious men of business, the Queen's wisest counsellors, seem to have realized how reckless this was.

Frobisher's fleet suffered an "outragious" storm, in which the ships were threatened by lumps of ice larger than themselves. One vessel was struck and lost with all her gear and stores, although the crew were saved. The High Admiral made a navigational error and entered what he later called Mistaken Straits, to the south of Meta Incognita.

There he encountered a strong tide race: "Many confessed that they found a swifter course of flood than before time they had observed. And truly it was wonderful to heare and see the rushing and noise that the tides do make in this place with so violent a force that our ships lying a hull were turned sometimes round about even in a moment after the manner of a whirlepoole, and the noyse of the streame no lesse to be heard afarre off than the waterfall of London Bridge."

Frobisher was in fact in Hudson Strait, and he penetrated it for 200 miles. He was enough of a sailor to realize that it was a more promising passage than the Frobisher Strait, which he had not explored further when instructed to do so. This time he obeyed instructions, turned about, gathered his scattered fleet and with all speed—for the ice was bad that year—filled his holds with the rocks of Meta Incognita.

In one particular, though, he fell short of his instructions. He had been ordered to leave a contingent to guard the mines. However, the prefabricated hut in which they were to live had been lost with the ship that had sunk, so the whole party sailed for home. On the way the *Busse of Bridgwater*, while separated from the rest of the fleet, sighted an unknown island and followed its coast for many miles. "Busse Island", as it was named, appears, from the description that the captain and crew gave, to have been a most desirable place; but its identity is a mystery.

Frobisher returned to England in the autumn of 1578 to find the Cathay Company on the brink of bankruptcy. Although there had still been no thorough test of the ore, everybody concerned had suddenly woken up to the fact that it was valueless, and this last cargo was dumped on the shore near Bristol. The shareholders who had paid for their stock lost their money and those who had not paid failed to answer Lok's appeals. He was soon in a debtor's prison, his wife and fifteen children short of bread.

Frobisher made no attempt to help him. He had, to his credit, stood aside from the discussion and excitement about the original sample and the later cargoes, and cannot himself be blamed for what was largely of Lok's own making. Besides, he was now having some difficulty in looking after himself. Though he had set out to become "famous and fortunate", he had meant to achieve this by finding the north-west route to Cathay, not by lading cargoes of ore—a role that did not suit him. Perhaps the role of explorer did not suit him very well either, for he was at his best when he had a definite objective—as when he participated, as vice-admiral, in Drake's expedition to singe the King of Spain's beard (his task was to render harmless the large Caribbean fort of Cartagena). In the North, his failure to recognize the magnitude and complexity of the Arctic's defences had led him to attack the first indentation he came to; and he simply did not know how to deal with a people who had never fought a war.

Frobisher would have a worthier place among explorers of the North-West Passage if on his first voyage he had at least tried to go on after losing his rowing boat, if on his second he had obeyed instructions and searched further west, or if on his third, he had persisted until his Mistaken Straits became identified with Sebastian Cabot's discovery. But it is unfair to blame him. The original purpose of the enterprise had been lost in a golden haze.

These voyages did, however, have one important result: in some way or other they caused the cartographers to change their ideas about arctic geography. The cartographers were a fascinating species: a mixture of the eternal inquirer, the modern journalist and what we now call the backroom boy. How they got their information no one knows, but it certainly was not only from official logs and published records. One pictures them talking with mariners, fishermen, whalers in port-side taverns, loosening tongues with liquor. They were by no means always right in what they drew, but sometimes they were inspired by what they heard. After Frobisher's voyages they no longer showed Asia as throwing out an arm above America. Instead they indicated a maze of islands straggling towards the Pole, which was much nearer the truth.

The Loss of *Fury*, a ship engaged in Parry's third expedition of 1824 (*Mansell Collection*)

Cutting into Winter Island, from an original drawing of the winter of 1821 on James Parry's second voyage in search of the North-West Passage (*Mansell Collection*)

Gale in the Pack 1842 (*National Maritime Museum*)

Sailing out of the ice (*National Maritime Museum*)

One of Sir John Franklin's ships, *The Erebus*, in the ice, in the 1846 expedition (*National Maritime Museum*)

Iceberg architecture. Natural beauty was something which explorers could appreciate only when they felt well equipped to cope with arctic conditions (*Scott Polar Research Institute*)

Bear hunting in the Arctic winter (*National Maritime Museum*)

Chapter 7

John Davis

For half a dozen years after Frobisher's third voyage, there was no apparent interest in the North-West Passage. Such interruptions and, after them, a tendency to start again from the beginning without full use of the data available are reasons why the search was so unproductive and, to a modern mind, inefficient.

Belief in the Passage remained among certain scholars and—to use that splendid word—cosmographers. But a fortuitous combination of circumstances was required to unite these individual urges and so create a force strong enough to launch another expedition.

John Dee was the most respected mathematician and geographer of the age. He had given advice during preparations for the voyage of Willoughby and Chancellor, and, when talk began of wider explorations, to rival those of Spain and Portugal, he coined the phrase "British Empire"—as a Welshman, preferring it to "English Empire". He was among those who held the view that America ended in the northern point of Labrador, but believed that there were "broken lands" (islands), not a projection of the Asian continent, between that point and the Pole. He was one of a commission of learned men who reported to Queen

Elizabeth that Frobisher's Strait was promising as a route to Cathay and that the cargo of ore that Frobisher brought back from his second voyage was, on the laboratory evidence, most valuable. This record suggests both wise and less wise counsel, and in fact Dee's end was sad, for he was carried away by too much study and became so deeply involved in the occult that an infuriated mob burned his priceless library, believing him to be in league with the devil.

But at the time we are considering he was the grand old man of geography. One evening in January 1584 he was entertaining Adrian Gilbert, youngest brother of Sir Humphrey, in his house at Mortlake. Adrian Gilbert, then in his middle thirties, was a doctor of medicine and a mathematician, and the discussion was on the North-West Passage.

Sir Francis Walsingham, Elizabeth's Secretary of State, happened to call in on his way downriver to Greenwich. He inquired the subject of the animated conversation that he had interrupted, and when this was told became so interested that he asked for a full exposition the next day.

To this meeting Adrian Gilbert brought his friend John Davis, a sea captain with something like twenty years of practical experience behind him and a reputation as a good navigator. Walsingham had been involved, at least as adviser to the Queen, over the Frobisher affair; but it is probable that he had never considered the North-West Passage from the viewpoint of men like Dee, Gilbert and Davis. At any rate, he was finally convinced that the search ought to be continued and that Davis was the man to lead it.

So far so good; but adventurers had to be found to finance the enterprise. In March, Davis and Adrian Gilbert laid their project before the Lord Mayor of London and three other men of the City. The meeting was held in the house in Mortlake of a merchant named Thomas Hudson, who was the uncle and guardian of a boy named Henry. It thus is more than possible that the young Henry Hudson, who years later would himself venture to the north-west, heard John Davis explain his plan. (The identification of this Henry Hudson with the explorer is not definite, however, though it seems likely.)

Davis was just the sort of man to capture a boy's affection and imagination—strong, enthusiastic, experienced, yet modest, patient and gentle. His temperament was almost exactly right for an explorer—the qualifying "almost" signifying a certain lack of hardness, though not of courage. This lack was more than counterbalanced by his ability to make friends, but other men did not always treat him well. One ran away with his wife during one of his expeditions (an occupational hazard with explorers) and others maligned him badly in later life. However, his likeability brought him many friends, and it was thanks to this that his first voyage to the Arctic was launched so easily.

The son of a yeoman, he had no more advantage of birth than Frobisher had; but from his schooldays he had been intimate with the three Gilberts (neighbours of his) and their close kinsman Walter Raleigh. The boys must often have sailed to Dartmouth together, and we may imagine them on the quay listening to the yarns of some old seaman and thus composing a picture like Millais's *Boyhood of Raleigh*. This close comradeship remained through life, providing Davis with the advantages of scholarship and a friend at Court. On the business side, the rich London merchant William Sanderson was married to a niece of the Gilberts. He put up most of the money for all three of Davis's Arctic voyages, and behaved as if he considered it a privilege to do so.

Not only did Davis's boyhood friends stick by him throughout life, but so too, it seems, did the men who served under him. We cannot speak with certainty of his crews, for their names are rarely recorded, but some of the few officers of his small fleet continued to sail with him even after his Arctic voyages were over. There is no more convincing tribute to a leader.

Davis is remembered as the first "scientific" explorer of the Arctic. His knowledge must have been mainly self-acquired, for he left Totnes school to go to sea before he was sixteen. But he learned enough to write in later life the *Seamans Secrets* and *Worldes Hydrographical Discription*, and to invent an instrument, the back-staff or Davis quadrant, which was an advance on anything until then available. There had been the ancient astrolabe (described by Chaucer), a thing of more metaphysical than navigational value; and Elizabethan seamen had used the cross-staff. This had roughly the shape of a cross of Lorraine and looked as though made by a carpenter. The observer, by holding the staff in front of him and moving one of the cross arms up or down the axis, could sight simultaneously on the sun and the horizon, thus measuring the angle. From the altitude of the sun at noon the latitude could be calculated. Accuracy depended on knowledge of the sun's seasonal declination, so the Pole Star was a better guide; but during the arctic summer a star is difficult to distinguish.

There was still no known way of calculating longitude. The sun, going round the world (apparently) in twenty-four hours, covers fifteen of the 360 degrees of longitude every hour. The longitude of a place therefore depends on the difference between Greenwich time and local time. But, even if he grasped this principle, an Elizabethan navigator could not know Greenwich time or calculate local time with sufficient accuracy. So only by latitude could he check his dead reckoning.

"Dead reckoning" meant calculating progress from speed and course. The vessel's speed was measured by means of the log ship (in effect a tiny sea anchor); the log line, which had knots at fixed intervals along it; and a half-minute sand glass. The log ship when cast over the stern remained virtually stationary in the water while the vessel sailed on for half a minute, and a counted number of knots in the log line were pulled overboard by the drag of the log ship.

The course was set by compass. The variation of the needle from true north could be measured by observing the Pole Star (when visible). Off the Greenland coast the angle of variation was about 30°, and, naturally, it was different in different locations. When a ship was keeping a steady course, dead reckoning could be reasonably accurate; but, when the ship was tacking against a wind, it was far less reliable. As has been said, progress north or south (latitude) could be checked by astronomical observations, but progress east or west (longitude) could not. It is scarcely surprising that as late as 1600 Frobisher Strait is shown in Greenland on contemporary maps.

Davis is remembered as a scientific explorer because he made the best possible use of the navigational aids and skills available to him. He made numerous entries in his log book every day, giving course, distance run, wind, elevation of the Pole Star, magnetic variation and any other point of interest. He had an ever-inquiring mind and was meticulous in his records.

His first expedition was well backed and consisted of two little ships, the *Sunshine* and the *Moonshine*. Setting out in June 1585, they were held up at the Scilly Isles for a few days by adverse winds. Never wasting a moment, Davis spent the time in charting the islands; then, as soon as the wind blew fair, set out north-westward.

After three weeks' sailing from the Scilly Isles, he made a landfall in south-east Greenland, Frobisher's Friesland. He was not favourably impressed, as his description of it shows: "mightie mountains all covered with snowe, no views of wood, grasse, or earth to be seen, and the shore two leagues off into the sea so full of yce as that no shipping could by any meanes come near the same. The lothsome view of the shore, and irksome noyse of the yce was such that it bred strange conceits among us, so that we supposed the place to be wast and voyd of any sensible or vegetable creatures, whereupon I called the same Desolation."

Bearing southward, he rounded the southern tip of Greenland, which he later named Cape Farewell. Then, turning north, he continued until he reached the fjord in which the present settlement of Godthaab is located. He named the fjord Gilbert Sound.

There he found a more kindly scene: many little islands on which grew grasses, flowers and ground berries. He made contact with the Eskimos, and greeted them with music and dancing. He was at great pains to be on the friendliest possible terms with the natives, and to assist towards this had taken on some musicians among his crew.

From Gilbert Sound he sailed north-westward in almost ice-free waters. Bearing west, he crossed the wide strait that bears his name (although he did not call it so himself) and reached Baffin Island. This he correctly took to be one of the "broken lands", and so set about searching for the Passage. He found what he called Exeter Sound, with Mount Raleigh on one side and Cape Walsingham on the other. He anchored in Totnes Road. Thus he decorated the unknown Arctic with the names of friends and Devonshire. He even found what he took (incorrectly) to be a primrose.

He examined the wide and promising Cumberland Sound, which is guarded by the Cape of God's Mercy; but adverse winds prevented him from reaching its head. The season being by this time well advanced, he turned for home, passing Cape Farewell.

Back in Dartmouth, he wrote with enthusiasm to Sir Francis Walsingham: "The North West Passage is a matter nothing doubtful, but at any tyme almost to be passed, the sea navigable, voyd of yce, the ayre tolerable, and the waters deepe." He went on to mention a possible trade in sealskins and whale oil. He was not the merchant impatient to find a trade route to the Orient. Solving the geographical problem was what mattered. But he was fully conscious—as only a poor man can be—that this would be costly; so he mentioned something that might help cover expenses.

He had reason to be optimistic. From study of the subject, from conversation with his erudite friends or by instinct, or by all of these, he had followed the right line. Instead of turning westward at the first opening, as Sebastian Cabot and Frobisher had done, he had first pressed northward.

In this he persisted during his subsequent two voyages, carefully charting the coastline as he went. He did not lack courage, but he was never rash; nor did he jump to conclusions. If Cabot and Frobisher had persisted they would have got themselves embayed, frozen in and martyred—in the wrong direction. Davis explored carefully, along the right lines. What finally stopped him after his third voyage was neither ice nor lack of persistence but a twist of history.

On his second voyage, in 1586, he followed the same general plan but on a wider front. He was more generously supported, being given, in addition to the *Sunshine* and *Moonshine*, the 120-ton *Mermaid* and the ten-ton pinnace *North Star*, along with pre-prepared materials with which to build another pinnace. He divided his fleet, sending the *Sunshine* and the *North Star* under Captain Richard Pope up the east coast of Greenland, while he with the other vessels went back to Davis Strait.

Pope's adventures do not concern us: he had no opportunity against the East Greenland current. Davis, on his side, faced stormy weather and took another fortnight to reach Gilbert Sound. There the materials for the spare pinnace were landed on an island and the construction was set in hand.

The Eskimos, inquisitive as children, gathered round to watch, arriving in a fleet of a hundred or more kayaks. "They hung about the boat with such comfortable joy as would require a long discourse to be uttered", Davis wrote in his journal. He encouraged them in every way, giving them knives as presents, visiting their summer tents of sealskin, making long excursions with them and compiling a vocabulary of their language.

But the Eskimos proved as mischievous as children. They began pilfering, and throwing stones at the sailors. Davis at first returned good for evil, giving more presents; but when they stole an anchor (they found metal objects irresistible) he took a native as hostage and, with him on board, sailed on when the wind blew fair. The anchor was lost, and the Eskimo soon died. They did not live in captivity.

It was a bad year for ice. Finding that the larger *Mermaid* was unhandy among the floes and bergs, Davis sent her home and continued his explorations in little *Moonshine*. He crossed his strait and surveyed the broken lands on the westward side between latitudes 67° and 57°. Besides revisiting Cumberland Sound, he located Frobisher Bay—which he called Lord Lumly's Inlet (for him Meta Incognita was in Greenland)—and coasted Labrador. His men caught many cod, with only bent nails and a sounding line as fishing tackle, and he brought home a fair cargo of sealskins bought from the Eskimos. It had been a comparatively unsuccessful voyage, but Davis was as hopeful as ever and determined to continue the search. He was ready to sell his beloved home on the river Dart to do so.

The West Country merchants fell away but Sanderson continued to back Davis and Walsingham to encourage him. In 1587 he sailed north with the *Moonshine*, the *Elizabeth* (of similar tonnage), and the *Ellen*, a little clinker-built pinnace. The intention was that the pinnace and the *Elizabeth* should fish, thus defraying some of the cost, while Davis explored in the *Moonshine*; but on reaching Greenland waters he showed more consideration for his backer's interest than for his own safety. He sent the two larger vessels off to fish while he continued in the pinnace.

The thin-planked sides of the *Ellen* were no match for the ice and she was soon leaking badly. There was murmuring among the crew. But Davis exhorted them to risk their lives rather than turn back, and on they went.

As a good leader he cared for the comfort of his mariners. When the work was unusually hard or the weather bad, he increased their rations. No variety was possible except by hunting and fishing. The basic diet was beef in barrels of brine, dried salted cod, bread and peas and plenty of beer. It cannot have been good beer, rolling in hogsheads on the Arctic seas; but the only alternative was water.

Sailing up the west Greenland coast, Davis reached latitude 72°—at that time, by far the most northerly point that a European had attained (the Vikings excepted). They hove to in sight of lofty cliffs. There was "no ice towards the north, but a great sea, free, large, very salt and blue, and of unsearchable depth". He named the place Sanderson his Hope of a North-West Passage—known for short as Sanderson's Hope. Prospects of success had never been so bright.

But a strong north wind sprang up in the night, driving the *Ellen* back and preventing her from passing latitude 73°. Then came the pack ice, herded by the wind into an enormous flock of floes and bergs stretching further than the eye could see. This phenomenon of the area became known as the Middle Pack. Once north of it there might, in a good season, be clear sailing; but it was impenetrable. That Davis tried to penetrate it—and with difficulty extricated himself—and then attempted to outflank it in a leaking vessel of twenty tons proves his courage and his power of leadership.

He now worked his way westward and then once more examined the coastline of the broken lands, coming at last to a place he describes as follows: "We fell into a mighty race, where an island of ice was carried by the force of the current as fast as our barke could sail. We saw the sea falling down into the gulfe with a mighty overfal, and roaring, with diverse circular motions like whirlepooles, in such sort as forcible streams pass thorow the arches of bridges."

As Frobisher had done in his Mistaken Straits, Davis had seen a tide race from the huge bay that Hudson was to explore. The place was later marked on maps as the Furious Overfall. Such names show that these men, however brave, were overawed.

Davis's experiences confirmed him in his belief in a northern route to Asia. On his return to England he wrote to Sanderson, "I have been in 73 degrees, finding the sea all open, and forty leagues between land and land. The passage is most probable, the execution easy." Whether the merchant would have backed him again we cannot know. Davis sailed from Dartmouth the following year against the Armada.

When the war with Spain was over he tried hard to launch another Arctic expedition, but Walsingham was dead and those in power were interested in other goals. He did become involved in an extremely ambitious project for approaching the Passage from the Bering Strait; but the voyage there was disastrously interrupted in the Straits of Magellan.

What did Davis achieve? In a sentence, he changed a vital sector of the Arctic from myth into reality. He established the relative positions of Greenland and the broken lands to the west. He charted 723 miles of the Greenland coast and roughly the same amount on the other side of his strait. Certainly he did not answer all the questions; but he left them clearly indicated. Even after a twenty-year gap, the next explorer had precise data to work on.

This gentle man of action with a scientific mind spent most of his latter years in writing, but not his last. Because of his skill as a navigator, he was in 1605 called from retirement to lead a trading voyage to the Far East by way of the Cape of Good Hope. Near where Singapore now stands he was killed by Chinese pirates. He would have passed through the same waters—though in the opposite direction—if one of his north-western voyages had succeeded.

Chapter 8

Cosmographers and Crews

North-western exploration in the seventeenth century not only depended on the sponsors but was initiated by them. In almost every instance they took the lead, deciding on a task and finding a man to fulfil it—a state of affairs that had not existed before. This remarkable generation of merchant adventurers deserves special mention.

The most active and enterprising individual was Sir Thomas Smith, a prosperous City merchant with a large house in Kent. He was known as Customer Smith because like his father he was a Farmer of the Queen's Customs. Before the turn of the century he was an active member of the Muscovy Company; and in 1600, when the East India Company was founded, by royal charter, he became the first governor of the new enterprise. He was several times re-elected and did not retire until 1621, four years before his death. That was one side of his life. The other was that he was deeply interested in exploration and arranged a series of lectures in his house. His memorials are a monument at Sutton-at-Hone, where he lived, and Smith Sound, at the northern extremity of Baffin Bay.

Sir Dudley Digges was much younger—less than twenty years old when the century began. Both a cape and an island in the Arctic are called after him. He was a country gentleman with a scholarly background and a taste for travel. He was a Member of Parliament and something of a writer, being the author of a publication on the East India Company and its ships, and *Of the Circumference of the Earth, or a Treatise on the North-West Passage.* He built a splendid house at Chilham, near Canterbury. He was a great family man. He had ten children.

Sir Francis Jones and William Cockayne were both City merchants and Lord Mayors with a private interest in exploration, while Sir James Lancaster was a man of action who commanded the first English voyage to the East Indies and the first voyage of the East India Company, of which he later became a director.

All these men had breadth of interest and depth of pocket and all in private life were students of the then particularly fascinating subject of charting the world. They might be called cosmographers as well as merchant adventurers. But there is another link: almost all were concerned with the East India Company. This great empire-building enterprise was successful from the very start, because it was run on sound business lines. But only two years after its inception we find in the minutes that the directors resolved, "this Company has an express interest in a voyage to discover a north-west passage".

Did these clear-sighted businessmen really believe, after a century of search, that the North-West Passage was a commercial proposition? "Express interest" strongly suggests it. Once their first ventures at finding the Passage had discouraged them as a corporate body, individuals among them still continued to give their backing to the search. Was it patriotism, the possibility of profit, a wish to see their names immortalized, or some other motive that made them do so? No doubt the adventurers' motives were as varied as the explorers'.

Among the most notable of those who helped to keep the stream flowing were Hakluyt and Purchas (Hakluyt's literary executor). As we have already seen, one of the banes of early exploration was the duplication of effort resulting from the loss, ignoring or misunderstanding of data. The Reverend Richard Hakluyt, born in 1553, gave his life to encouraging the study of navigation and collecting accounts of exploratory voyages (mainly English), from the earliest times to his own. His *Divers Voyages Touching the Discoveries of America* was published in 1582 and his monumental *Principall Navigations* in 1588. Until his death in 1616 he "continued", as he said, "to wade still further and further in the sweet studie of the historie of cosmographie" and "to incorporate into one body the torn and scattered limbs of our ancient and late navigations by sea". Another churchman, Samuel Purchas, continued the record, in *Haklutus Postumus, or Purchas his Pilgrimes.*

Hakluyt, who carried out his researches in conjunction with a full ecclesiastical career (he was archdeacon of Westminster when he died), was interested in the motives, as well as the achievements, of exploration. He was a recorder, not a commentator, and so did not directly discuss the matter in his works; but a study of his thousands of pages shows the focus of his interest. He searched for patriotism as a motive, and did not always find it. He invariably paid generous tribute to the sponsors. What of the captains and crews? Hakluyt printed the accounts written by the Elizabethan captains, or those that their officers wrote for them; most of our information on their exploits comes from the pages of the *Principall Navigations*. To find out their motives we must read between the lines, taking each case separately.

About the crews, being a generality, it should be easier to generalize. They were a fine and hardy body but had their Achilles heel of selfishness and cowardice. One may wonder why those who were responsible for the strikes and mutinies that occurred, who complained at conditions or balked at the terrors of the Arctic, should have volunteered for service in the cold and dangerous North, for all mariners were paid more or less the same, whatever the desination. Patriotism, the chance of private trade (some trinket to be bartered for a valuable fur, say), and thoughts of the tales they would be able to tell afterwards may all have played a part in inducing them to go. However, one must not forget that it was a time of high unemployment, or fail to make allowance for the variety and fallibility of men.

Since paid crewmen were so fallible, were amateur adventurers better? This breed is first recorded on Frobisher's voyages. There was the hope of gold, of course, but the "gentlemen" seem to have behaved well. In an intensely class-conscious age, they rolled up their sleeves and dug for dross alongside miners and mariners. One speculates whether crews made up of amateur adventurers might have been better.

It seems that Hakluyt was interested in this question, since he took pains to record in detail an amateur adventure. As this account is interesting not only in the present context, but also as an example of Hakluyt's style (in this case he is not merely recapitulating), it is worth quoting from at length.

One master Hore of London, a man of goodly stature and great courage, and given to the studie of Cosmographie . . . encouraged divers Gentlemen . . . to accompany him in a voyage of discoverie upon the Northwest parts of America: wherein his perswasions tooke such effect, that within short space many gentlemen of the Innes of court, and of the Chancerie, and divers others of good worship, desirous to see the strange things of the world, very willingly entred into the action with him . . . .

From the time of their setting out from Gravesend, they were very long at sea, to witte, above two moneths, and never touched any land untill they came to part of the West Indies about Cape Briton, shaping their course thence Northeastwardes, untill they came to the Island of Penguin . . . .

M. Oliver Dawbeny . . . told M. Richard Hakluyt of the middle Temple [cousin of the historian] that lying there they grew into great want of victuals, and that there they found small reliefe, more then that they had from the nest of an Osprey, that brought hourely to her young great plentie of divers sorts of fishes. But such was the famine that increased amongst them from day to day, that they were forced to seeke to relieve themselves of raw herbes and rootes that they sought on the maine: but the famine increasing, and the reliefe of herbes being to little purpose to satisfie their insatiable hunger, in the fields and deserts here and there, the fellowe killed his mate while he stooped to take up a roote for his reliefe, and cutting out pieces of his bodie whome he had murthered, broyled the same on the coles and greedilyd devoured them.

By this meane the company decreased, and the officers knew not what was become of them: And it fortuned that one of the company driven with hunger to seek abroade for reliefe found out in the fieldes the savour of broyled flesh, and fell out with one for that he would suffer him and his fellowes to sterve, enjoying plentie as he thought: and this matter growing to cruell speaches, he that had the broyled meate, burst out into these wordes: If thou wouldest needs know, the broyled meate that I had was a piece of such a mans buttocke. The report of this brought to the ship, the Captaine found what became of those that were missing, & was perswaded that some of them were neither devoured with wilde beastes, nor yet destroyed with Savages: And hereupon hee stood up and made a notable Oration, containing, How much these dealings offended the Almightie ... and besought all the company to pray, that it might please God to looke upon their miserable present state, and for his owne mercie to relieve the same .... And such was the mercie of God, that the same night there arrived a French ship in that port, well furnished with vittaile, and such was the policie of the English, that they became masters of the same, and changing ships and vittailing them, they set sayle to come into England.

The last sentence is surely a masterpiece of diplomatic description. Hakluyt rode 200 miles to get this story from the last member of the party still alive.

From this horrific instance we move on to the first voyages sponsored by the East India Company, with hired captains and professional crews.

In May 1602, George Weymouth sailed from England in command of the *Discovery* (seventy tons). He was "thoroughly victualled and abundantly furnished will all necessities for a yeare and a half". It was an expensive expedition.

Weymouth's account of the voyage is as vague and confusing as the fog in which he generally found himself as soon as he was across the Atlantic and north of Newfoundland. He explored the Labrador coast, looking for a channel that might lead him to the west.

On 18 June he sighted Greenland and on the 29th Warwick's Foreland, on the other side of Davis Strait. It appears that, owing to wind and ice, his course was very erratic. On 1 July, to quote from his account, "the winde was at West, with fogge and snow; the ayre being very cold. This day wee came into many Overfals, which seemed to runne a great current; but which way it did set we could not well discerne . . . ."

On the 19th, "the winde was at North and by East, and our course to the Eastward. The same night following, all our men conspired secretly together to beare up the helme for England while I was asleepe in my Cabin . . . ."

Captain Weymouth called a council of his officers and the Preacher, the Reverend John Cartwright, who had bought himself new vestments for use in Cathay. These gentlement did not support their captain. On the contrary, they set down in writing their argument that he should retreat and start again next season.

"Then, wee being in the latitude of 68 degrees and 53 minutes," writes Weymouth, giving a remarkably high latitude, "the next following, about eleven of the clocke, they bare up the Helme, being all so bent that there was not meanes to persuade them to the contrary. At last understanding of it, I came forth of my Cabin and demanded of them, who bare up the Helme? They answered me, One and All. So they hoysed up all the sayle they could, and directed their course South and by West."

Weymouth says he did some more exploring on the way home. But it is all misty. One can scarcely imagine a less successful expedition.

In spite of an understandable lack of enthusiasm on the part of his colleagues, Sir Thomas Smith managed to launch another north-western expedition in 1606. The forty-ton *Hopewell*, with John Knight in command, anchored somewhere off the northern end of Labrador on 26 June. She had suffered damage from collision with an iceberg, was leaking and had a broken rudder. John Knight his brother, the mate and three men went ashore. They carried surveying instruments and were well armed. They walked over a hilltop and were never seen again. That was effectively the end of that expedition. It was popularly supposed that they had been eaten by the cannibal savages. Tudor myths and imaginings persisted into Jacobean times.

To explain the next voyages we must first introduce a totally new patron and briefly digress in time. Christian IV of Denmark and Norway was conscience-bidden to find relics of the old Norse colonies in west Greenland. England comes into it because this descendant of the Vikings felt it necessary to send to England for captains and pilots, and our theme is concerned because interest was again directed to the area that Davis had explored.

The Vikings, of course, had not searched for the North-West Passage. If they had, they might quite possibly have found it, for nothing could stop these men in their beautiful open boats. While other seamen still hugged the shore—in much bigger vessels—they sailed out across the ocean and let the land drop below the horizon behind them. They would no more have mutinied than they would have missed a chance of pillage. They were wild and lawless, courageous to the point of foolhardiness, hardy to a degree beyond our comprehension. But they had never heard or dreamed of Cathay, and, although Englishmen in their Litany had prayed to be delivered from the Norsemen, they had not yet read the sagas. Except perhaps as port-side legend the story of the Norse transatlantic voyages was not known. It cannot have directly influenced John Cabot's decision to sail west.

In the year 986 Eric the Red had occasion to leave the Norse colony of Iceland in a hurry, having committed murder there. He led a fleet of twenty-five ships, crowded with whole families and their domestic animals. The fourteen open boats that survived rounded the southernmost cape of a new land and found harbour in the deep fjords on its south-west coast. The twelfth-century historian Are Frode says of Eric that "He gave the land a name and called it Greenland, and said that having a good name it would entice men to go thither."

This earliest recorded example of travel publicity was successful. Shiploads of colonists came from Iceland, which is largely ice-free, to Greenland, 85 per cent of which is covered by permanent ice. Supply and trade ships came from Norway. In the land that Davis called Desolation they created a colony with, at its peak, sixteen churches (Christianity followed the first settlers), 280 farms and about 2,000 people. They discovered America in the year 1000, and later obtained timber from the St Lawrence area, for there were only dwarf willows and birches in Greenland.

These restless men probed northward—much further than the English explorers so far mentioned. An inscribed stone has been found in latitude 72° 55′ North, beyond Sanderson's Hope. An account written by Priest Hallder in 1246 speaks of a voyage that evidently penetrated Smith Sound to a latitude higher than 80°. On Washington Island in Smith Sound there is a tall cairn built by men unknown.

In the year 1410 the yearly intercourse with Norway ceased. By 1600 it was realized that all the colonists had long since died. The reasons attributed were the Black Death, the interruption of communications by the maritime monopoly of the Hanseatic League, and massacre by the Eskimos. None of these in itself is adequate. These people had learned how to live off the land and water, but, cut off from all communications with Europe, they would lose hope, become in-bred, gradually weaken. To survive, let alone prosper, the colonists had to work ten times harder than the agriculturists of fertile Europe.

We are left with an inscription found much later near the present Julianshaab, and that in translation reads,

> Vigdis, daughter of Magnus, rests here
> May God gladden her soul.

They all rest thereabouts—from south to north along the Greenland side of Davis Strait and Baffin Bay.

King Christian's expedition, with Danish mariners and mainly English officers, discovered nothing of archaeological interest. In fact they were soon diverted from their original purpose by finding igneous rocks that shone with silvery flakes. It happened to be gneiss (a word derived from the Old High German *gneiston*, meaning "sparkle"), a rock usually composed of quartz, felspar and mica. When the expedition of 1605 brought back specimens of this, two more were despatched to collect cargoes.

They also hijacked five Eskimos complete with kayaks. The urge to obtain live specimens of this strange species still persisted, and it is not to be supposed that any account was taken of their feelings. Back in Elsinore a boat race was organized. The kayakers easily beat all the others; but this cheered them not at all. They were desperately homesick. One of them was moved to tears whenever he saw a woman and child, and they all tried to escape and cross the ocean to Greenland in their tiny craft. They were overtaken and brought back, and soon afterwards they died.

When the gneiss proved to be what it was, King Christian lost active interest in the fate of his ancestors. The most important result of the voyages he sponsored was that an English captain, James Hall, made a probe northwards along the Greenland coast, taking William Baffin as his pilot. Baffin, after apprenticeship elsewhere in the Arctic, was destined to follow up and greatly expand the explorations of the next pilgrim with whom we shall have to deal, Henry Hudson.

Chapter 9

The Wanderings Of Henry Hudson

While the unfruitful expeditions described in the last chapter were taking place, the Dutch had been busily and profitably engaged in the north-east. The English Muscovy Company may not have been much concerned by Barents's discovery (or rediscovery) of Novaya Zemlya and Spitsbergen, but that the Dutch had become firmly established in Archangel and seemed in a fair way to discovering the North-East Passage worried them considerably. The high prices in Britain suited the merchants: they had money to spare; and considerable unemployment meant that crews could be easily recruited. The Muscovy Company looked round for a captain and navigator.

They chose Henry Hudson, presumably because he was the best man available, though we know nothing of his career till that date. This is unfortunate, as Hudson is the most puzzling, yet probably the best remembered, character in the whole saga of the North-West Passage. How could he achieve this niche of fame while being, apparently, so vacillating, temperamental and unheroic? He discovered (among other things of importance) an inland sea with which much of the rest of this record will be concerned. If only for this reason, he deserves in our search for motive as close an analysis as we can give him.

The only definite records of his life cover the period from 19 April 1607—when, before setting out on what we presume to have been his first voyage to the Arctic, he led his ship's company of nine men and a boy (his son John) to take Holy Communion in the church of St Ethelburga in Bishopsgate—to 21 June 1611 when he was cast adrift by mutineers. Besides that there are only surmises and sidelights.

It will be remembered that in 1584 John Davis and Adrian Gilbert met a number of City men at the house of one Thomas Hudson, who was uncle and guardian of a boy named Henry. There is no proof that this boy was the explorer to be, but the likelihood that it was may explain Henry Hudson's obsession with the North-West Passage, something that may thus have been the goal of his ambition from his early youth. It was as though he had in his head a compass that forever pointed north-west. Set him off in any direction and he would swing to that quadrant. Only when he frankly aimed north-westward did he persist to the end.

There is reason to believe that Henry Hudson had a house near the Tower of London, was married to a woman named Katherine and had three sons. The second of these, John, accompanied him on all his Arctic voyages. Hudson was not a merchant; he did not attempt even minor trading in the lands that he visited, and, indeed, went ashore only once or twice in the course of four voyages. His interest was in major questions of geography, not in detail. Presumably he was a sailor by profession, a navigator who worked for merchants. He certainly had read the accounts of Davis's exploration, and perhaps Davis and he had corresponded. His first voyage was made only two years after the death of Davis, who was an active letter-writer to the end. All Hudson's voyages were intended to reach Cathay. Two were made for the Muscovy Company, one for its Dutch equivalent, and the last under the sponsorship of private individuals. He more or less kept to the letter of his instructions, but his changes of course were often illogical—unless one explains them as obsessional orientation.

The First voyage, in the *Hopewell*, was intended to cross the world over the centre of the Arctic Ocean. The rationalization of this plan depended on a thesis expounded to Henry VIII by Robert Thorne, a near-contemporary of Sebastian Cabot. Thorne had presupposed that "there is no land uninhabitable and no sea unnavigable". He had gone on to argue that the North Pole, "that place of greatest dignity on earth", was warmer than the surrounding regions. He was in fact correct, because (as he did not know) the Pole is in the sea; but he was irresponsibly wrong in supposing that the climate there was temperate and the area of the Pole ice-free. Yet, other theorists, including a contemporary of Hudson's, the Reverend Samuel Purchas, Hakluyt's successor, had supported Thorne. Purchas argued that, as the meridians were far apart at the equator and at the Pole met in "a Point, but Nothing but Vanitie", the best way across the world was across this vanity. The power of rational thinking had not advanced much during the century since Thorne had worked out his theory.

Hudson's first voyage inevitably failed in its main object. He ran into the impenetrable defences of the pack ice. But it is interesting that he had at once trended to the westward, to the Greenland shore; and the fact that he felt it necessary to justify himself in so doing suggests that the due-north route intended was not of his own choosing.

"It may bee objected against us as a fault, for haling so westerly a course", he wrote. "The Chief Cause that moved us thereunto was to see that part of Groneland, which (for ought we know) was to any Christian unknown; and wee thought it might as well have been open sea as land, and by that meanes our passage might have beene the larger to the Pole."

From the Greenland coast he turned north-eastward and followed the ice-front all the way to Spitsbergen, where he cruised about—it seems rather aimlessly—for a month. He then retraced his course westward before returning home.

Apart from providing information on the quantity of whales and morses (walruses) in Spitsbergen waters, the voyage achieved nothing positive. The factual statements in the log show that Hudson did everything possible to press northwards, but they do not suggest any heart-felt urge to reach and pass the Pole, nor belief that it might be done.

Hudson was as conscious of the hand of God as were any of his predecessors. After pressing boldly into a lead of open water and, when it closed, failing to tow the *Hopewell* backwards out of it with the ship's boat, he recorded, "Here we would have finished our discoverie, but in this extremitie it pleased God to give us a small gale at north-west by west, we steered away south-east four leagues . . . . God give us thankful hearts for so great a deliverance."

Hudson wrote in the Elizabethan manner, being by birth and upbringing an Elizabethan. His belief in God was matched by his appreciation of the Creator's inanimate works. What is striking is that he chose as members of his crews men who did not fear God, nor the devil. Either he did not care deeply about the religion so eloquently expressed or he cared still less about people, having no time for their idiosyncrasies. It is difficult to believe that he could otherwise have shown such a lack of insight into character.

He could not be faulted on his conduct of the voyage, and his information that there was a wealth of whales and walruses launched a tremendous industry of slaughter. The Muscovy Company once again made something on the side. They were quick to commission him for another voyage in the *Hopewell*, this time to find a North-East Passage.

Hudson replaced his entire crew except for his son John and two mariners of whom we know nothing, James Skrutton and John Cooke. This would appear to contradict what has just been stated—except that, with one exception, he did not choose better men. His new mate—a post that is vital to morale—was Robert Juet. He was an oldish fellow from Limehouse, a grumbling Jeremiah given to pessimistic prophecies. Hudson took him on his last three voyages, as he did Arnold Lodlo, Michael Perse, and Philip Staffe, who was the carpenter and the only man worth his salt.

Such a radical change of crew suggests that there had been trouble on the first voyage. There is no hint of this in the log, which in its remaining form is a copy made by one of the sacked mariners, John Playse. He faithfully recorded such mysteries as the dip of the compass needle, which must have been beyond his comprehension; and, if there were any derogatory passages that he might have preferred to omit, why did Hudson make him his copyist? Thus early there are question marks. But the cast of the final tragedy is already being collected.

The log of the second voyage is in Hudson's own hand; so we may trust it, as far as it goes.

The *Hopewell*, this time with a crew of fourteen, left St Katherine's on the Thames on 22 April 1608, and made a slow, cold, rough passage to the north-eastward. On the morning of 15 June, when she was in latitude 75°, about halfway between Norway and Spitsbergen, a "mermaid" was seen by two of the crew. Hudson was sufficiently interested to question the two men closely and made what for him was a long entry in the log.

"One of our companie looking over board saw a mermaid, and calling up some of the companie to see her, one more came up, and by that time shee was come close to the ship's side, looking earnestly at the men: a little after, a sea came and overturned her; from the navile upwards, her back and breasts were like a woman's, her skin very white; and long haire hanging downe behinde, of colour blacke; in her going downe they saw her tayle, which was like the tayle of a porpoise, and speckled like a macrell."

The editor of the Hakluyt Society's collection of Hudson material dismisses this incident with the footnote "Probably a seal." However, it deserves closer attention: first from the point of view of men's credulity, and second from that of discipline.

The editor, secure in the modern conviction that if a creature is unknown to science it does not exist, presumes it was a seal; but Hudson and his men were less inhibited. There are several roughly contemporary records of mermaids. None was ever seen combing her hair. (Presumably they would be too considerate of the hawksbill turtle, from which "tortoise-shell" is made.) One mermaid, found on the shore of Belfast Lough, was domesticated and baptized—whether as Catholic or Protestant is not stated. Another, found flapping her tail in the mud on the wrong side of a Dutch dyke, was taken to Haarlem and taught to spin. A third was caught off Borneo and lived for a week in a vat. She would take no food but left excretions like those of a cat. Hudson's men could believe in such things, but only one of them had sufficient curiosity to come on deck to see what another had sighted. Not even the boy John was stirred. Were they being seasick (there had been a lot of "sickness") or were they too busy with their gallon of beer?

This brings us to the second and more important point—discipline. On a vessel of eighty tons in unknown waters only one man was on deck. He must have been the helmsman. In such circumstances a cry of the helmsman is an order that the watch on duty, the mate and captain must instantly obey. Yet only one mariner came up.

At this stage of maritime history even minor breaches of discipline were savagely punished. The boatswain swung his heavy whistle as a weapon; men were ducked from the yard arm, manacled, put in the bilboes (stocks); and flogging was so common that "some sailors do believe in good earnest that they shall never have a fair wind until the poor boys be duly whipped every Monday morning."

There is no record of Hudson ever punishing anyone (except by demotion on his last voyage) or praising anyone either. One cannot help thinking of a professor absorbedly working out a theorem on the blackboard without a thought of what is going on behind his back.

Continuing north-eastward, the *Hopewell* encountered ice on 18 June. There had been none three days earlier when the mermaid was seen, which is interesting, for a seal cannot swim for long without resting on a floe. But the ice, when reached, proved impenetrable for the ship, as it had the year before on the other side of Spitsbergen. So Hudson swung righthanded towards Russia.

Almost connected with the Russian coast is Novaya Zemlya, a cucumber-shaped land mass 600 miles long, and consisting of two main islands and some minor ones. On a modern map it separates the Barents Sea from the Kara Sea. There were three possible ways by which Hudson might pass this obstacle: by rounding its northern point, by passing between its southern end and the continental coast, or by finding the passage between the two main islands (the Matochkin Shar). Hudson decided to look for the passage through the middle, which was marked on the chart made by Barents; but he made his landfall 200 miles south of this and did not expend much time or effort in searching.

Near the southern end of Novaya Zemlya the crew spent a good deal of time hunting walrus. They were not good at it. A walrus is as big as an ox but on land scarcely more mobile than a rocking horse. Yet of hundreds seen on one island, only one was killed. Hudson allowed all his men to go after them, remaining on board with only his son. This surely was rash or weak. The crew, for their part, were keen enough to hunt, for the hides would have had value as harness leather and the tusks as ivory. However, not long after the men had returned, the ship was almost overwhelmed by drifting ice and saved only "by the mercie of God and his mightie help".

The crew brought back information about the waterway off which they were anchored. Hudson had taken it for a river mouth, but he was told that "the great river or sound was of a breadth of two or three leagues and had no ground at twentie fathoms, and that the water was of the colour of the sea and very salt, and that the streame setteth strongly out of it". This evidence suggested that the "river" was a passage through to the Kara Sea.

Up came the anchor and they sailed in. "Wee all conceived hope of this northerly river or sound, and sayling in it wee found three and twentie fathoms for three leagues. . . . Then the wind veered more northerly and the streame came down so strong that we could do no good on it: we came to anchor and went to supper"—a mess of ducks and geese shot in this paradise for migratory waterfowl. Then the mariners slung their hammocks in the odd corners they had staked out for themselves, and the captain went to his cabin.

We may wonder what his thoughts were that night. He had advanced nine miles and the soundings were still over twenty fathoms, very deep for a river. Moreover, the water remained salt even when the tide ebbed. Where could it come from except the Kara Sea? As an intelligent man it would occur to him that if this was the keyhole of the North-East Passage he had happened upon it as fortuitously as had Frobisher on his "strait". That might be explained by the guiding hand of God, but it remained for him to obtain the final proof. If things were as they appeared to be, his expedition would be an outstanding success; and he could see no other explanation.

We do not know the workings of Hudson's academic mind, but we do know what action he took. The next morning he sent off Juet, his idle and grumbling mate, with five men in the ship's boat. They were provided with weapons and sufficient food to press on until they obtained the final proof. Hudson did not go himself, as Davis would have done: he remained in his cabin.

It is possible to identify the waterway on a Russian chart of 1937. It is called Kostin Shar. It is not a river, but a horseshoe-shaped channel (average depth about fifteen fathoms) that curves northward and then west to re-emerge in the Barents Sea. In fact it is a passage round an island. This might have been proved by Juet in a day of good sailing or two or three days rowing; but the channel has a very promising branch that runs due east, with depths of up to twenty-one fathoms and deep water near the shore. It is actually a dead end, but the whole Kostin Shar would take at least a week to explore thoroughly. Juet was absent for about thirty hours, and lied about the little that he saw.

At noon the next day he returned to say that throughout twenty miles the waterway had steadily shallowed until it was only one fathom deep; so they had landed for the night "and found a good store of wilde goose quills, a piece of an old oare and some flowers". These he brought back to the *Hopewell*. They were all that Hudson brought back from his search for a North-East Passage.

Hudson's log records, "We presently set sayle . . . and we stood out againe to the southwestwards, with sorrow that our labour was in vaine." And later, "We . . . stood to the westward, being out of hope to find a passage by the north east." His behaviour suggests that he had never had much hope of or even interest in it.

During the first week of July he searched for Willoughby's Land. This is a land of which mention had been found in the record recovered from the dead ships off the Lapland coast in 1554. Sir Hugh Willoughby had explored further eastward before being frozen in on his way home. He had sighted new land. Almost certainly he had seen what half a century later was called Novaya Zemlya, which means New Land. Sea captains of the Muscovy Company had yearly looked out for it on their devious sailing routes to Archangel. Hudson could not find it because he had just left it. So he continued to the west, or west-by-south.

On 27 July he was near the Lofoten Islands, off the west coast of Norway. This is mentioned in the laconic log because for the first time they had to light a candle in the binnacle, there having been perpetual daylight until then. With fair winds the crew might have expected to be in English waters within a fortnight.

But Hudson did not intend to go straight home. The Lofoten Islands entry goes on to recall the reasons why he had turned back from Novaya Zemlya, and concludes, "I therefore resolved to use all meanes I could to sayle to the north-west considering the time and meanes we had, if the wind should friend us, as in the first part of the voyage it had done, and to make triale of that place called Lumleys Inlet and the furious overfall by Captain Davis, hoping to runne into it an hundred leagues and returne as God should enable me." There could not be a clearer, bolder statement of intent—however unpractical at the end of July.

There follows an eleven-days break in the log—a record that every skipper keeps as a matter of duty every day—and then a entry dated 7 August: "I used all diligence to arrive at London, and therefore now I gave my companie a certificate under my hand, of my free and willing return without persuasion or force of any one or more them."

There could scarcely be a clearer indication that there had been persuasion or force, and furthermore that the captain undertook that there would be no victimization. Hudson justified his action—before himself, one feels—by recording that the winds had not been favourable and that it was too late in the season. "I thought it my duty to save victuals, wages and tackle by my speedy return, and not by foolish rashness, the time being wasted, to lay more charge upon the action." In other words, surely, he thought there would be a better chance next year.

But soon after his return to England it began to look as if he would not get another chance. The Muscovy Company were interested in whales and walruses, but not in any more geographical exploration, for the moment at least. The Dutch were, however. They were recovering their wealth and power now that they were no longer in the grip of Spain. The Dutch East India Company, which had been formed in 1602 with the enormous capital of half a million pounds, offered a reward of 2,500 florins to anyone who should discover for them a shorter route to the Orient. By this they meant the North-East Passage. Their agents held many discussions with Hudson—his friend Jodocus Hondius, a sculptor, engraver and map maker, acting as interpreter. The negotiations dragged on and on. Either the Dutch were not quite sure of their man or they were chiefly concerned to prevent him from exploring for anyone else.

Finally Hudson, who *had* to get a ship somewhere, offered his services to the king of France. This may have been bluff, but subtlety is not apparent in his character—oversimplicity, rather. In any case, the Dutch East India Company immediately signed him up.

"Tied him up" might better describe it. The company contracted to "equip a small vessel or yacht of about thirty lasts burden [sixty tons], with which, well provided with men, provisions and other necessities, the above named Hudson shall about the first of April, sail, in order to search by the north, around by the North side of Nova Zemla, and shall continue thus along the parallel until he shall be able to sail southward to the latitude of sixty degrees". He was instructed "to deliver over his journals, logbooks, and charts, together with an account of everything whatsoever which should happen to him during the voyage without keeping anything back." For this service he was to be paid £65, and if he should die upon the voyage his widow would receive £16 in full settlement.

> In matters of commerce the fault of the Dutch
> Is giving too little and asking too much.

Although it was not laid down in the contract, it was agreed that a Dutch mate and half a dozen Dutch seamen should be included in the crew. This, as it turned out, was where the company was over-subtle.

Hudson sailed in the *Half Moon* on 25 March 1609. On 5 May the ship was off the North Cape and on an east by south-east course. This we have from Juet, whose record is the only first-hand account remaining. Hudson's own log-book has been lost: presumably it was sent to Holland after the voyage. Juet was serving in a position that was officially subordinate to the Dutch mate. His account is sketchy and vague, particularly so at this interesting stage of the voyage. His next entry refers to much wind and snow on 19 May, and states, "We made our way west and by north till noon." They were heading in a north-westerly direction, and there is no explanation.

The Dutch consul van Meteran wrote in subsequent correspondence that the Dutch sailors mutinied. They were accustomed to southern seas and disliked handling frozen ropes and sails. It is not to be supposed that Hudson put up much opposition to the *Half Moon's* being turned back but it is a little surprising that he did not then continue towards the Furious Overfall. (He had the relevant charts and papers in his sea-chest.) Perhaps the Dutch sailors objected to the North West Passage as much as to the North East. Perhaps there was a second mutiny. At any rate, having called at the Faroe Islands, kept a look-out for Busse Island, and passed the French fishing fleet on the Newfoundland banks, Hudson turned further south, towards the American coast.

A detailed account of this third voyage would be justified only on the assumption that Hudson believed that the river now called after him might be a channel cutting through to the Pacific. Captain John Smith had written to him from Virginia that the Indians believed there was such a channel in that area, and Hudson certainly explored the tidal reaches of the Hudson river much more thoroughly than he had explored the Kostin Shar. But, if ever he hoped that it might prove more than a water highway to the interior, it cannot have been for long. So this voyage, which led to the founding of New Amsterdam, later to be called New York, concerns us only as regards character.

Juet, although in a subordinate position, appears from his account to have dominated the ship's company. He was light-fingered with pistol and culverin where the Indians were concerned and killed a good many of "the treacherous savages", Hudson was on friendly terms with them, went ashore and shared their food. On the other hand, he acquiesced in the killing or, at least, is not recorded to have taken steps to prevent it. The carpenter, Philip Staffe, got on with his job. He cut one of the splendid trees and made a new mast for the ship. We do not hear anything about the Dutch mate and sailors.

The *Half Moon* sailed for England on 4 October and dropped anchor in Dartmouth on 7 November. Hudson immediately sent a full account to the Dutch East India Company and asked them to back another voyage—in search of the North-West Passage.

Chapter 10

Hudson's True Purpose

The Privy Council paid Hudson the negative compliment of forbidding him to go to Holland. Though they were preoccupied with trying to prevent the king from obtaining too much money through his divine right and had nothing to spare for a voyage of discovery, they did not want Hudson to give his services to another country.

His reputation had never been so high. In his three voyages he had been to Spitsbergen, which was further north than Davis had been, had visited the mysterious Novaya Zemlya, which blocked the North-East Passage, and in the west had found a rich and fertile land. It was this last that held the strongest appeal for the public. Feeling it right that the Dutch should be the first to hear the result of their expedition, Hudson had ordered his crew not to talk of the voyage. Consequently that was what everyone wanted to know about. The Muscovy Company were interested in him again. But in the event Sir Thomas Smith, Sir Dudley Digges and Sir John Wolstenholm gave their personal backing for a voyage in search of the North-West Passage, and Henry, Prince of Wales, the enterprising and independent-minded youth who visited Sir Walter Raleigh when King James had had him put in the Tower, and who, had he lived longer, might have been

Britain's Henry the Navigator, gave his patronage. This was strong sponsorship.

Appropriately, the barque with which Hudson was provided was named *Discovery*. A less happy augury was that she had been Captain Weymouth's ship. Hudson made a number of changes in his crew, replacing some of the English and all the Dutch. But he kept the worst and the best: Robert Juet, the mate, and Philip Staffe, the carpenter. The rest were a strange mixture. The quartermaster was John King, rough and illiterate but honest enough. Robert Bylot was a new hand. He was an experienced seaman and a fair navigator—far better qualified than Juet; but, as a character, he needed careful handling—the more so, perhaps, as he was given no official position. Arnold Lodlo and Michael Perse had served Hudson twice before without particular distinction; and there were two Wilsons, unrelated and utterly unlike, except that each added a dangerous ingredient. William Wilson was a savage, foul-mouthed Barnacle Bill; Edward Wilson was a surgeon aged twenty-two. From much the same cultural stable as Edward Wilson came Thomas Wydowse, a young intellectual who is described as a mathematician and who seems to have signed on for adventure in the modern sense of the word. Also from a non-maritime background and not directly in pursuit of his profession, if it may so be called, was Abacuk Prickett. He was a house servant of Sir Dudley Digges, and probably this scholarly country gentleman had put him forward as someone sufficiently articulate to give him sidelights on the voyage.

Those are nearly all the speaking parts among the crew who left St Katherine's on 17 April 1610; but there is one silent actor who must be mentioned—John Hudson. If anything he said had been recorded, or if anything he wrote remained on record, he might have entirely altered our conception of his father and the detail of his voyages. He must have known his father's mind as he must have known the crew's. But he is the most noticeably silent of all the silent cabin boys. Perhaps someone somewhere may find a letter from him to his mother.

One most articulate crewman joined the *Discovery* only at Gravesend and therefore was not on the register—presumably he had his wages paid by Hudson, not by the sponsors. This was Henry Greene. Hudson has already appeared as a bad judge of character, but this choice suggests something more positive, a kink at least. Greene, though strong and intelligent, was a morally degenerate waster. He blasphemed quite openly, which was something in those days. He had lived with and on prostitutes. His respectable parents had disowned him.

Hudson, whose writings are full of God's grace, took him up. In the brief interval between voyages, November to April, he invited him to live in his house. Mistress Hudson and John's two brothers had seen little of Henry during the past three years, and now he planted a waster on them. He himself must have been very busy at this time with the Dutch East India Company, the Muscovy Company, and his final backers, as well as with the equipping and provisioning of his ship. Yet he found time to obtain from Greene's mother a decent suit of clothes for her son; he promised to use his influence with Prince Henry to get this young man appointed to his guard; and—most extraordinary of all—he took him on the voyage that was to fulfil or destroy his life's ambition.

Greene got into some sort of trouble at Harwich. "He should have gone into the field with one Wilkinson", wrote Abacuk Prickett in his journal. As to his meaning, we can be sure only that it was derogatory, for as a great Bible reader Prickett disapproved of the atheist.

Greene again caused trouble in Iceland, where the *Discovery* was held up for a fortnight by bad weather. He has a fight with the young surgeon Edward Wilson. This was damaging to morale because the crew took sides; Hudson took Greene's, saying that Wilson had "a tongue that would wrong his best friend". Juet hinted darkly in his cups that the captain had put Greene on board as a spy. Hudson did not hear of this remark until they were at sea again. Then he was so angry that he nearly turned back to put the mate ashore—nearly, but not quite. He pressed on for the Furious Overfall.

He rounded Cape Farewell and headed westward. According to the information he possessed that was the right direction. His data were that Sebastian Cabot had found the "North-West Passage" in about 62° North; that Frobisher had penetrated his "Mistaken Straits" and experienced a whirlpool like "the waterfall of London Bridge" in the same latitude; and that Davis had found the Furious Overfall in what appeared to be the same place. Latitude at least could be depended on. Hudson headed west, towards what Cabot and Frobisher had believed was the gap between the continents of America and Asia, and Davis between America and the broken lands. Cabot had stated that an arm of the Pacific Ocean opened on that strait. Frobisher had been more guarded, since his partial penetration had been owing to a mistake in navigation and was against instructions, and he had already committed his name to a bay that he had called a strait. Davis had noted the same tide race, but had not investigated further.

Davis's map had given Hudson a general indication of the coastline, but there remained that unmappable factor, drift ice. Ice and fog kept Hudson wandering uncertainly for many weeks. There is no need to follow his course precisely; his changing mood is well enough expressed by the place names he bestowed. The first land seen after crossing Davis Strait he called the Isle of Good Fortune. It should have proved so, for it was Resolution Island, at the mouth of the strait for which he was looking. But fog blinded and ice jostled him. He wandered into Ungava Bay (on the south side of the strait) and out of it again, naming an island Desire Provoketh, a headland Hold with Hope and some barren rocks where he sheltered the Isles of God's Mercies. Only when at last he had found his way throughout the whole length of what we call Hudson Strait and had before him the huge expanse of Hudson Bay did he use the names of two of his patrons. Cape Wolstenholm was the 2,000-foot cliff in which the mainland of Ungava ends;

Cape Digges was a 1,000 foot cliff on an island (also called after Digges) two miles from shore. They were painted white by seabirds and shimmered with their tireless movement. Such was the dramatic gateway by which Hudson entered his bay.

The crew had no doubt bestowed their own names, or at least epithets, on the features they had passed. There had been much discontent. In Ungava Bay this had been openly expressed, and Juet had mocked at the captain's assurance that they were sailing to the East Indies. Hudson had reacted to this indiscipline with sweet reason at first, bringing out his chart and explaining the course. This had had little effect. The men thoroughly disliked this "great and whurling sea", and said so. Then Hudson, in one of his rare forceful moments, asked them point blank whether they wanted to go on or turn home. One sailor answered that if he had a hundred pounds he would give ninety to be back by his own fireside. At this Philip Staffe broke out that he "would not give ten of it to be back in England", but on the contrary, would consider it "as good money as ever he had any".

Hudson himself, after a long period of doubt, was certain that he knew where he was—and was wrong. He believed that the North-West Passage was comparable to the Straits of Gibraltar and that he had passed through it. The hundred-year-old error persisted. He was at that moment convinced that the sweep of water opening before him was part of the Pacific. He was impatient to reach Cathay.

He was so impatient that, when a party sent ashore to examine Digges Island reported not only birds and deer but also stone caches of game left by the Eskimos, he would not pause to replenish his food stocks but sailed on.

"So we left the fowle, and lost our way downe to the south-west", Prickett noted later, no doubt thinking of what he would tell Sir Dudley Digges. But during the next few days there can have been no indication that the captain had lost his way. He held a southerly course fast and purposefully for over 500 miles. Probably he had turned into Ungava Bay near the beginning of the strait thinking he had already gone far enough westwards. Now that he was convinced of it he pressed south with confidence and in a hurry to reach warm water.

He reached the shallow, desolate, dead end of James Bay.

Then, "Up to the north wee stood till we raised land, then down to the south, and up to the north, then downe again to the south."

The modern map of Hudson Bay is an evocative picture. Here was this single-purposed man driving on beyond the point of no return in search of his life's ambition. The only possible exit to the west is right up in the North between Foxe Basin and the Gulf of Boothia. It is a narrow passage as easily blocked by the enemy as the Suez Canal. It has never been found in a navigable condition. To the south, east and west there is nothing but Canada.

Still holding to his hopes but already nagged by doubts, Hudson gave his last exhibition of firmness. He had broken off his log-book—or else it was destroyed by mutineers. (They saw to it as well as they could that nothing should remain that might be used as evidence against them.) We depend mainly on Prickett's journal. But of this incident there are some notes left by the mathematician, Thomas Wydowse. They must have been overlooked when his belongings were ransacked. They are brief but to the point.

Hudson accused Juet of disloyalty. The mate demanded an open trial before the whole crew, but the witnesses (some of them future mutineers) destroyed his defence. Mathues, the cook, stated that when they had first sighted Iceland Juet had said that "the action", the voyage, would "prove bloodie for some". He went on to say that Juet had recently threatened to turn the ship round and take her home.

Philip Staffe and Arnold Lodlo kissed the Bible and spoke up for the captain, the latter adding that Juet had told them to keep swords and loaded muskets in their cabins because they would be needed before the voyage was done. Wydowse concluded with what was presumably his own opinion, whether expressed at the trial or not. "Wee being pestered in the ice, hee [Juet] had used words tending to mutinie . . . jesting at our master's hope to see Bantam by Candlemasse."

Hudson replaced the mate with Robert Bylot. Francis Clement, the boatswain, was also degraded—in favour of Bill Wilson—because he "had basely carryed himselfe to our master in the action". The wages thus saved went to Wilson and John King, the quartermaster. It is not stated that Bylot got any more pay by his promotion.

With characteristic final leniency—unlikely to be appreciated—Hudson promised Juet and Clement that if they behaved themselves in future their bad behaviour would be forgotten.

At that moment he was evidently still in command of his crew; but he did not know where he was. He was at the southern extremity of what is called a bay but is in fact an expanse of almost-landlocked water over three times the area of the British Isles. Still he had no intention of turning back, even if he could have re-passed the Furious Overfall. It was Bantam by Candlemass—or winter in the ice. He told no one of this determination but continued to search the area of James Bay "for some reason to himselfe knowne", as Wydowse put it.

In his dogged, silent determination he appears increasingly to have lost balance, and authority. Knowing the end we can foresee it. This dedicated explorer was killed less by the vastness of his self-imposed task than by a series of small human errors and weaknesses not unlike those we know so well in ordinary life.

At the end of September he found a good harbour, but he at once sailed out of it again for some reason to himself known, impatience perhaps. They ran into bad weather and had to anchor in an unsheltered place. After a week of storm, the

wind moderating but the sea still high, Hudson decided to weigh anchor. As everyone may not now know clearly, the anchor was raised on the principle of winding
a grandfather clock, lifting the weight by turning the capstan. On this occasion, at
the moment when the anchor came clear of the mud, the ship lurched violently in
the waves. The anchor-weighted cable ran out again, spinning the capstan in
reverse and throwing two men across the deck, hurting them badly. We may be
sure that every mariner said that he had known something like that was bound to
happen.

Philip Staffe, who on his own initiative was standing by with an axe, cut the
hemp cable, and thus prevented greater loss. He is apt to appear as the prototype
of the good sailor. It would be fairer to describe him as one of the few who
compulsively speak their minds in any circumstances. They make themselves unpopular by generally being right, but not always. They are their own executioners.

Sailing on, Staffe told the captain that if he held his course he would hit a rock.
Hudson, who recently had been sure enough of himself to bring out his chart and
discuss it, could no longer accept advice. They ran on a rock and were aground for
twelve hours. Then the rising tide lifted them free, as Prickett noted, "by the
mercy of God unhurt but not unscarred". Neither was the captain's prestige left
unscarred.

The tiresome carpenter suggested that it would be wise to build a hut on the
shore. Hudson rejected what would in effect have been admission of defeat.

The gunner, John Williams, died from natural causes. It was maritime custom
to sell a dead man's clothes by auction. In those conditions clothing mattered
almost as much as food. Before the days of oilskins, only the stoutest woollen
garments gave protection and the gunner had left a homespun gaberdine smock.
Hudson autocratically awarded this to Greene, who had received a trousseau
worth £5 (six months' livelihood in terms of wages) just before departure. Of
course, he may have bartered this for drink or women in Iceland and been in rags;
but Juet's drunken remark about Greene's being the captain's spy must have been
remembered.

At the end of October Hudson suddenly decided to winter where he was—in
the south-western corner of James Bay. He sent Prickett and Staffe ashore to find
a suitable site. (It should be noted that he did not go himself.) The footman and
carpenter had little choice. Digges Island and Cape Wolstenholm, which they
might still have reached, were swarming with non-migratory birds, and there
were the Eskimo food caches there; but Hudson was not going back, was staying
in the sump of the great bay, where the water shallowed gradually to a flat and
marshy shore. The rough grasses must already have been bent double by the first
wet snow, the dwarf willows laden with it. A few hunchbacked conifers expressed
their dejection and silently prophesied a wind-swept winter. But there it had to
be—where the North-West Passage ought to have been.

The *Discovery* was towed as near as possible to the shore and in less than a fortnight was frozen in.

This was the first time that an English crew had faced a winter in the North—unpremeditated, unprepared for, and short of food. Now was the time for leadership. But Hudson was not a leader; his natural place was at a gaming table. On his calculated prediction he was ready to stake his life, and those of everyone with him.

But at the moment he had not even a table. The ship, grounded in shallow water, was no doubt on her side. Hudson sent word (note that he sent word) to Staffe to build a hut. The carpenter sent word back that he could not. He had good reason: the ground was by this time frozen, making it difficult to drive in stakes, and in freezing weather metal sticks to the skin. Any good carpenter holds spare nails in his mouth as any good seamstress holds pins; but below zero these tear off the skin.

Hudson, hearing that Staffe "neither would nor could goe in hand with such works . . . ferreted him out of his cabbin to strike him, calling him by many foule names, and threatening to hang him".

Staffe walked off the ship and went shooting. Hudson had encouraged hunting by offering a reward for game brought in, but had stipulated (for better safety, though to the disadvantage of successful hunting) that men should go in pairs. The companion whom Staffe chose was Henry Greene. This irrationally infuriated Hudson, who told Greene he was a waster and worse and gave the dead gunner's gaberdine to Bylot.

While this row was going on, Staffe took his box of tools ashore and built some sort of cabin. But it was a bad beginning to winter. Food was short and they were cooped in a little hut. Hudson must have resented the crowding crew, and they his aloof presence. Bylot was on his side and Staffe was steady. There was little opportunity to talk in private. A cold peace was maintained. They subsisted largely on ptarmigan, partridge-like birds that offer their white breasts to the worst shot time and time again; but the meat is insipid without seasoning and it is unlikely that there was enough of this available. The ice-bound crew had an unhappy Christmas. Any beer remaining must have gone off if it had not already turned to vinegar.

In the early spring the great armadas of ducks and geese touched down briefly, and left again for their Arctic breeding grounds. These thousands upon thousands of banquets in the sky cannot have improved morale.

So early summer came, and the intolerable strain of waiting for the ship to be freed. Long before the ice melted, the swarms of mosquitoes and black flies appeared. The insects of northern Canada can drive men mad. Frogs also appeared. The hungry men ate these, and moss.

In the previous autumn they had seen the footprints of a Man Friday in the snow. Throughout the cold and hungry winter they had been haunted by the thought that human beings lived in this wilderness, knowing how to hunt its animals. When the snow was melting an Indian walked calmly into camp. Hudson had been feasted by the Indians on his *Half Moon* voyage, and hoped to be now. He gave this Indian a knife, some buttons and a mirror. The Indian indicated that he would return after a few sleeps.

He did so, this time dragging a sledge with two deer skins and two beaver skins on it. He offered back the presents he had been given and indicated that he came to trade.

It was meat not skins that Hudson wanted; but he was at his worst at this time, and for some reason offered half the barter price that had been asked. The Indian, dignified, inscrutable, accepted without argument, but he did not come back again. A ship may never have been lost for a hap'orth of tar, but on this occasion a captain condemned himself for the equivalent.

Hudson went in search of the tribe, guided by the smoke of their camp fires. They avoided him. After a few days he returned frustrated.

It is unlikely that during these few days the men left behind did not search the ship. They could not get into the hold without breaking the locks, but hungry men, like hungry mice, can smell cheese. Hudson had in fact—perfectly legitimately and properly—kept back a store of food. The concern and conversation of the mariners, put at its best, must have been that this store should be used for getting them home, not for a continuing search for the non-existent Passage.

Picture Hudson returning thwarted from his useless attempt to make contact with the Indians, faced by a crew with something on their minds. He quarrelled with Bylot, his only valuable ally besides the quartermaster John King, honest but illiterate and completely unqualified. This rearrangement having been made, the *Discovery* set sail.

For what destination? The captain's log having been discontinued or destroyed, it is impossible for us to answer this vital question; nor could the crew, for the new mate could not navigate. If they had accepted that Hudson was taking them home, they would surely have had no reason for complaint, for he was as skilful as anyone alive; but they thought he was continuing his search for the Passage, and they may well have been right. He steered north-west.

At the same time this mystery of a man divided the reserve of biscuits with his own hand—one pound each. "And hee wept when hee gave it unto them." The chronicler will be recognized by his biblical style. Their net had brought up "fourscore small fish, a poore relief for so many hungry bellies".

Abacuk Prickett was in his bunk with painfully swollen joints, a symptom of scurvy. Adam Moore was still suffering from the effects of the capstan accident. Syrake Fanner was another casualty. Henry Greene was also laid up, writhing in agony, for Hudson had issued the last fortnight's ration of cheese, good and bad together, and Greene had eaten it in one meal. But after two or three days he was up again, as hungry and angry as ever.

One more small foolishness of Hudson must be recorded, and an over-honest answer by Philip Staffe. The captain, having distributed the food, believed that the crew had a secret hoard. He sent the ship's boy round to search the sea chests, and Nicholas Symes found about thirty loaves. Why should not the men keep something to go with their small fishes? The resentment can imagined. The crew, on their side, believed that Hudson had secret access from his cabin to the hold. Bill Wilson questioned the carpenter, who replied that "it was necessary that some of them should be kepte uppe". Everyone had been given an equal ration, but—Orwell would have a phrase for it.

The drama swept up to its crisis on the night of Saturday 23 June, while the *Discovery* lay moored to a floe. She was a comparatively large ship and several of the men had separate quarters. As in the incident of the mermaid, there was no watch on deck, and now there was not even a helmsman. Where there is drift ice and no wind the sea is generally as still as a lily pond. We can imagine absolute quiet. Most of the ship's company were asleep, but, as Prickett later noted, "wickedness sleepeth not".

Henry Greene and Bill Wilson came into his cabin. They were the ringleaders. It is fortunate that they thought Prickett worth preserving if they could suborn him, for otherwise we should have no record

Greene and Wilson told him that the resolve was to put Hudson and the sick men into the shallop, the ship's boat, to fend for themselves, and then to sail home. Prickett, it was made plain, would be cast away too unless he were prepared to speak up for the mutineers on their return to England. This feudally loyal, pious, weak-willed, sick man was faced wth this in the middle of the night, 3,000 miles from home.

He appealed to their better natures, of which they had none. Greene told him (to put it in modern parlance) to shut up. He himself preferred to hang than starve, he said. He was going through with the action while it was hot.

Prickett says he said, "I did not join this ship to forsake her, nor to damage myself and others by such a deed." To which Greene answered, "In that case, you can take your chance in the shallop."

Prickett took up the Bible at his bedside and said, "You shall sweare truth to God, your prince and countrie: you shall doe nothing, but to the glory of God and the good of the action in hand, and harme to no man."

Greene and Wilson took the vague oath as lightly as they would have spat. John Thomas, Michael Perse, Bennett Mathues, Adrian Motter, and Juet came in and did likewise.

"The will of God be done," said Prickett.

Left alone, he lay in his bunk, the blasphemed Bible by his side. No doubt he listened in the silent ship.

At last Bennett Mathues, the cook, rattled his pans as he went to the butt to draw water for breakfast. That was the signal.

When John King appeared he was at once accosted. On some pretext he was got into the hold and bolted down. Philip Staffe was engaged in conversation. Hudson, coming out of his cabin, was seized and bound by Wilson, Thomas and Mathues.

Hudson's first reaction appears to have been amazement. He demanded of his captors what they intended. They answered that he would know whan he was in the shallop.

Henry Hudson, one of the great explorers, has been analysed critically; but in this moment he towered above his mutinous men. In a flash, seeing the riff-raff that constituted so large a proportion of his crews, one realizes the magnitude of his achievements, and the tremendous odds against which they were achieved. The mutineers wanted him dead, wanted the invalids dead because they could not work for their food, wanted to silence any with a sense of loyalty; but they had not the courage to kill them outright. They preferred that they should die, slowly and painfully, out of sight. We must not say that they were bestial, for beasts do not behave like that.

The shallop was drawn up alongside and Hudson with his son bundled into it. Prickett, who was watching, mentioned no sign of fear. The captain was wearing a multi-coloured dressing gown, which makes the scene all the more bizarre. The sick men were dragged from their bunks and thrown into the boat. John King was sent after them because he was honest. So was Wydowse, the intellectual, whom they could not understand and therefore mistrusted. This was not even a well-planned mutiny. They threw Mathues and Thomas into the boat—the men who with Bill Wilson had gripped and bound Hudson. Only at the last moment did they have them out again and replace them with Lodlo and Butt, who were not noticeably on one side or the other.

All this happened in a few mad moments. Then Philip Staffe, not particularly quick-witted, broke free of those who had detained him and drank in the situation. He was useful; they wanted to keep him as insurance. He told them to wait a minute and went below. He reappeared with his box of tools, his musket, an iron pot and a bag of meal. He went aboard the shallop of his own accord, saying that he preferred to commit himself to God's mercies than to the hands of such villains. The mutineers cut the boat adrift and started looting.

Throughout all this, Bylot had kept below, out of the way, but he later stated that the shallop was last seen heading into the depths of the bay. If so, Hudson made no attempt to get back to the Eskimo food caches on Digges Island which he might just conceivably have reached. Evidence was later found that he had pressed onward.

Chapter 11

The North-West Company and William Baffin

In the second decade of the seventeenth century the flood of interest in the North-West Passage ran strongly, and in two channels. The Danish-sponsored expeditions to Greenland, particularly James Hall's probe northwards along the coast, kept alive the search along that line. But Hudson's last voyage concentrated attention on the great bay that he had partially explored, and it is appropriate to look first in that direction.

Within days of their crime, the mutineers were struck by a thunderbolt from heaven. As soon as they had found their way back to Digges Island—which they did with difficulty—a boat party went ashore to shoot birds and to trade for venison with some Eskimos who had appeared and who seemed friendly. Suddenly the natives attacked them with harpoons and arrows. John Thomas, Michael Perse, Bill Wilson and Greene were killed, and although Prickett managed to stab his assailant to death he received "a most cruel wound" himself. These were heavy casualties for the already self-depleted crew.

With 300 birds as provisions, they sailed for England. They would never have got there had it not been for Bylot, who had kept below during the mutiny but came up to take command. He interpreted the Sixth Commandment as Clough did later:

> Thou shalt not kill: but need'st not strive
> Officiously to keep alive.

But he was a tough and competent seaman.

It was a nightmare voyage. Long before they sighted Ireland they were existing on bones fried in candle grease. Juet died "for mere want" and the rest of the crew sank into useless lethargy. Bylot had to navigate, steer, trim the sails alone.

But, once back in England, Abacuk Prickett came into his own. The servants'-hall lawyer and the competent seaman who had saved the ship went at once to report to Sir Thomas Smith. They made an effective team. We cannot know what lies they told, but it is probable that they took with them Hudson's "card", or survey. It was much the best ever made of that quarter of the Arctic, for Hudson was expert in his profession. It delineated very clearly what had been seen. But it left the western side of the Bay blank—because this had not been seen. Therefore it might be deduced that there was no western coast but instead a continuous waterway to the Pacific—a conception all the easier to believe because it had been held since the time of Sebastian Cabot. At any rate, Smith and his fellow adventurers appear to have been more interested in prosecuting exploration than mutineers.

The Masters of Trinity House held an inquiry and gave it as their opinion that the men ought to be hanged. But this was not a legal judgement, nor did the inquiries held by the High Court of Admiralty result in one. In fact, no real trial was held until seven years later. Then Prickett, Edward Wilson, Mathues and Clement—only these—appeared in court on two charges, of the ejection and murder of Hudson and others, and of fleeing from justice. There is no account of the proceedings, only the verdict of the jury: Not Guilty on both counts.

During these seven years much had happened. Soon after the *Discovery* had limped home, in 1611, the Company of Merchants of London, Discoverers of the North-West Passage was formed. Its seal incorporated the ostrich plumes of Prince Henry. The Governor was Sir Thomas Smith. The Directors included Sir Dudley Digges, Sir Francis Jones, Sir James Lancaster, Sir John Wolstenholm and Sir William Cockayne. Among the long list of members appeared the names of Richard Hakluyt, the Earls of Salisbury, Southampton and Nottingham, and Robert Bylot, Abacuk Prickett and Edward Wilson.

In May 1612 the *Resolution* and the *Discovery* were sent to Hudson Bay under the command of Captain Thomas Button. Bylot and Prickett were in the *Resolution*, and possibly Wilson also.

There exists no first-hand account of this expedition, only the version given by Luke Foxe; but it does not appear that any attempt was made to find signs of the men who had been cast adrift in the shallop the year before. From Digges Island Button sailed westward until he was stopped by the further shore of Hudson Bay. He explored it down to the mouth of the Nelson river and there he wintered. Although provisioned for eighteen months, and lucky in their ptarmigan shooting, his party suffered severely from scurvy and the cold. When his ships were released from the ice the following June, Button returned to England.

His negative report did not discourage the North-West Passage Company. The next year, 1614, they again sent off the *Discovery*—that "good and luckie ship", as Purchas for some reason described her—on another voyage in the same direction. Captain Gibbons, the commander, with Bylot as mate, got no further than a bay in Labrador. He remained there so long from stress of weather that his crew called the place Gibbons his Hole. He returned to England in the autumn without having accomplished anything. But still the enthusiasm of the company was un-abated. Belief in Hudson Bay, particularly its north-west corner, was strong.

We must now turn briefly to the other channel of interest, Davis Strait. As has been said, James Hall, while working for King Christian, had in 1605 made a sortie up the Greenland coast—to 69° North. In 1612 he recieved backing from Sir William Cockayne and Richard Bell to take the *Patience* and *Heartsease* on a similar voyage.

The chief importance of this expedition is that it is where William Baffin makes his entrance on the historical stage. We know nothing about his origin. Purchas describes him as "that learned-unlearned mariner and mathematician, who, wanting art of words, so readily employed himself to those industries, whereof here you see so evident fruits". This surely suggests that Baffin was self-educated. A study of his work gives a number of hints that he started at the bottom of the ladder. To climb to the top in that age was a great achievement. But, as to his present fame and popularity, the complete edition of his *Voyages*, stamped when received by the Cambridge University Library on 19 September 1881, still had its pages uncut when the present writer took it out.

Baffin signed on at Hull as pilot of Hall's *Patience*. She and the *Heartsease* sailed in April 1612. Reaching Greenland, the *Patience* anchored in Davis's Gilbert Sound, then called Hope Harbour and now Godthaab, while Hall and Baffin, transferring to the *Heartsease,* continued up the coast and explored as far as Cunningham Fjord in 67°. They then turned back to Holsteinborg, then called Rommel's Fjord. This was where the five Eskimos had been kidnapped by the Danes seven years before. Hall had played no part in the abduction, but he had been on board the ship concerned and no doubt had been seen by the natives, and was remembered.

Going ashore with a party of English mariners on this second occasion, he was met by a company of Eskimos. These took no notice of the mariners but one of them walked straight up to Hall and harpooned him at close range, killing him.

Apart from that tragic incident, this was a successful expedition. The outstanding result was the number and accuracy of the observations made by Baffin. Besides his duties as pilot he was deeply interested in magnetic variation and the dip of the needle and made the first painstaking attempt to find longitude in the field. It took him more than a day and was approximately accurate.

After his first Greenland experience, Baffin made two voyages in Spitsbergen waters for the Muscovy Company—still under the enormous umbrella of Sir Thomas Smith. These added considerably to his reputation but do not otherwise concern us. Baffin's post was pilot. He commanded none of the several ships concerned.

In 1615 he returned to the service of the North-West Company and made two voyages with Robert Bylot. The association of these veterans—for they must both have been middle-aged (old-aged in terms of exploration), and had both already made three voyages to the Arctic (counting Bylot's twenty-week sojourn in Gibbons's Hole)—is most interesting. They met aboard the old *Discovery*, which had made one more Arctic voyage than either of them.

They evidently got on excellently, although Baffin—by far the better mind, the better explorer, and with quite as much sailing behind him—was in the secondary position. Bylot was a thoroughly experienced seaman, no more nor less. Baffin was much more—a maritime scientist in the morning of that age (Davis was at the dawn). Each had the intelligence to appreciate the other and comprehend what he could give. They wanted different things. It was a case of temperaments being sufficiently dissimilar not to clash.

Although inevitably there is some guessing, in this lies the analysis of an interesting situation. Bylot was a touchy man with a small yet urgent ambition. He had started as a common seaman and done some studying because he wanted a handle to his name. As such he joined Hudson's exploratory voyage, with its long chances. Having proved his worth (Juet the opposite), he was promoted. Then he was demoted, not from any professional failing but through a personal quarrel with Hudson. That accounted for his base yet not culpable behaviour in the mutiny; he was never charged. He brought the good ship and the bad company home. This depended primarily on Ancient Mariner toughness plus knowledge of the direction of the British Isles and the ability to take a rough latitude.

It sufficed to restore his self-esteem and provide him with a reputation. He was considered worth taking on two voyages, as the only man who knew the way.

In 1615 he became Captain Bylot. This was the height of his ambition. But he was far from sure whether he could justify that lonely and imaginative responsibility on a voyage of exploration into unknown waters. Therefore he accepted the rank while implicitly handing over the responsibility to his pilot. Here by an extraordinary stretch of chance he was lucky, and one hopes he realized it. He behaved as though he did. He left Baffin to direct the course of the voyage, to take all the observations, to write the log and keep the journal. He, presumably, looked after day-to-day discipline and the set of the sails. But he was the master in name only. His pilot directed every exploratory detail of the voyages.

This suited Baffin perfectly. He seems to have been deaf to the call of ambition, listening only to the commands of his vocation. This may seem to be idealizing him. Baffin *was* an idealist, probably without realizing it himself. Not only did he navigate and make remarkably accurate maps; his magnetic observations—not demanded by the North-West Company—made it possible for Professor Hansteed to complete the first magnetic chart a century later. It must be borne in mind that the vagaries of the compass were a serious cause of worry to navigators in that era. The Magnetic Pole, as opposed to the North Pole, was still a mystery.

Although no botanist or zoologist, Baffin listed the plants and animals he found. He described the Eskimos, their kayaks and oomiaks. He was a compulsive observer and recorder.

Geographically, he concluded on the first voyage that Hudson Bay did not offer the best opportunity of a passage to the Pacific. He carefully explored the north-west corner in the vicinity of Southampton Island, and deduced—from the depth of water, the tides and currents, the ice and the trend of the land—that there was no practicable passage in that quarter. He returned to England without losing a single life, an unusual achievement at that time.

The late Vilhjalmur Stefansson once remarked that the story of a really well-run expedition contains no adventures. Baffin's accounts contain no brushes with the Eskimos, shipwreck, mutiny or disaster, and therefore are not exciting reading—except in the context of the developing search for the North-West Passage. On his final Arctic voyage, in 1616, having rejected the possibilities of Hudson Bay, he sailed north through Davis Strait and beyond. He had started un-usually early in the season, in March, and by the end of April was at Sanderson's Hope. There, where Davis had found "a great sea, free, large, very salt and blue", Baffin was beset by ice.

After jousting with the Middle Pack, he found a way past it near the Greenland coast and attained his farthest north in a channel that he named Smith Sound, in honour of his chief patron. He was only on one occasion able to land on the icebound shore. He did not know that Smith Sound was the direct route to the Polar Ocean (he would have had to get much further to do so), but he described the place as "admirable" in that the compass variation there reached 56°, "a thing almost incredible and matchless in all the world beside".

He sailed southward on the western side of what was to be known as Baffin Bay, passing and naming Jones Sound and Lancaster Sound, after his other patrons. He had been in the very antechamber of the North-West Passage, but did not realize the supreme importance of these sounds. Being unable to enter them because of ice, he thought that they were bays.

Apart from exploration, he was anxious to get ashore, for scurvy had broken out and claimed two lives. But with ice still obstructing him he finally crossed over to the Greenland coast and anchored in Cockayne Sound. There scurvy grass (*Cochlearia officinalis*) was gathered. Boiled in beer and served with sorrel this restored the sick men to health. The boiling of the scurvy grass even in so laudable a liquid must have reduced its efficacy, but the sorrel (*Oxyria reniformis*), eaten as salad, no doubt added to it. This expedition, made in the year of Hakluyt's death, achieved much more than any had done previously or was to for two centuries to come. There is significance in this 200-year-long gap. Baffin charted the great bay, larger than Hudson Bay, that he first explored and was too modest to call after himself. He certainly indicated the sounds in their correct positions. We know his thoroughness and still have his map of Hudson Strait and the northern part of Hudson Bay—an admirably clear piece of work.

We have not his map of Baffin Bay. All his material went to Purchas, as the literary executor of Hakluyt. Purchas published a letter from Baffin to Sir John Wolstenholm and his *Briefe and True Relation* of the voyage—from which the facts given have been taken. But, instead of publishing the scientific data, Purchas noted, "This map of the author, with the tables of his journal [log book] and sailing were somewhat troublesome and too costly to insert."

It is best to give the results of the omission in the words of the nineteenth-century chronicler and traveller Sir Clements Markham, who felt very strongly about it.

"It led to such confusion in the ideas of mapmakers that at last the very existence of Baffin's Bay was doubted. On the map of Luke Foxe 1635 it is shown correctly. But Hondius published a version quite different from the reality, and others followed him. In Moll's Atlas (1720) both the correct delineation of Luke Foxe and the very erroneous one of Hondius and his imitators are given. Van Keulen and D'Anville caused still greater confusion. In the Maltebrun atlas (1812) there is a slight improvement. Daines Barrington gives what he calls 'a circumpolar map according to the latest discoveries.' He treats Baffin's Bay as a semi-circular dotted line with '*Baffin's Bay according to the relation of W. Baffin in 1616 but not now believed*' written across it. Finally in Sir John Barrow's *Chronological History of the Voyages to the Arctic Regions* (1818) Baffin's Bay is entirely expunged, Davis Strait being made to open northwards on a blank space. Thus, owing to the omission of the map and log by Purchas, the great discovery of Baffin became at length entirely ignored and discredited."

To complete Baffin's personal story, he at last achieved a command, of the *London,* in the East India Company's fleet. In 1622 his ship was part of an English force engaged in reducing the fort of Kishm on the Persian coast, then held by the Portuguese. Captain Baffin went ashore to measure the distance and height of the walls "for the better levelling of his guns". One can imagine him absorbedly setting up his instruments. He was hit by a bullet and killed instantly. Thus, like Davis, he died in the East, which he had tried to reach by sailing north-westward.

The resurrection of his reputation as an explorer did not come about until 1818, when Sir John Ross rediscovered his bay and paid tribute to the accuracy of his fixings, particularly of the mouth of Lancaster Sound, the vital corridor.

But 200 years of exploring time had been wasted—and a unique opportunity lost.

Chapter 12

The Wrong Turning

There always have been individuals ready to risk their lives to find out what lies beyond the horizon, but fairy godfathers are rarer. The merchant knights continued to grant the wishes of explorers for the first three decades of the century, and there was peace. The opportunities were ideal; but effort was misdirected.

Since we must follow history, we must follow the ships, leaving assessment and speculation until the end of the era. In 1619 King Christian sent the *Unicorn* and the *Lamprey* into Hudson Bay under the command of Jens Eriksen Munk, a captain in the Danish navy. He encountered a great deal of ice, and, having at last reached what is now Port Churchill, on the west shore of the bay, decided to winter there.

Munk was a careful leader. He set his men gathering ground berries and hunting ptarmigan, but scurvy with its symptoms of loosened teeth, painful joints and general enervation took a terrible toll. By the time the snow had gone, in the following June, only Munk and three others remained alive, crawling about on hands and knees in search of something green to eat. They had given up hope. But when the ice began to melt they were able to catch fish; and then, slightly strengthened, managed to put to sea in the *Lamprey*, the smaller vessel, and sail home.

After this gallant disaster there was a pause of ten years. Then we have the first example of two rival expeditions in the field at the same time. One was led by Luke Foxe, who sailed from London, the other by Captain Thomas James from Bristol. The ports are significant. Bristol had had its merchant adventurers, under whatever name, before the days of John Cabot—that was why Cabot went there. They had been foremost in trade with Iceland, in developing the Newfoundland fishing, and in searching for other (mythical) lands in the western ocean. But London had taken the lead and kept it. It was from London, or Hull, that the ships of the North-West Company had sailed. The Devon Ports had dropped out, but between the others there was enough rivalry to stimulate endeavour.

Luke Foxe was born in Hull and educated—in all that concerns us—in John Tappe's bookshop in London (Tappe specialized in matters maritime). His most valuable friend was Henry Briggs, the professor of astronomy who introduced the practical use of logarithms—and introduced Foxe to the influential diplomat Sir Thomas Roe. Through him Foxe gained access to Trinity House and Sir John Wolstenholm, and so finally achieved his lifelong dream of leading an arctic expedition. That was his motive, the fulfilment of a romantic ambition conceived in childhood. He had trained himself for it. He was "sea-bred since Boyes-days", having studied navigation and read everything in print about the North.

He was still in his "Boyes-days" when he unsuccessfully applied for the post of mate on Knight's expedition of 1606. Such presumption was typical of him. He had the highest possible opinion of North-West Foxe, as he called himself. He persisted in his ambition until, twenty-five years later, he was given the use of HMS *Charles*, an old eighty-ton gunboat up for sale. It was on hearing of this that the Bristol merchants fitted out the *Henrietta Maria* under the command of Captain James. Thus, apparently by coincidence, the two vessels bore the names of the reigning king and queen. The king subscribed no money to either enterprise, but he gave each of the explorers a letter for the emperor of Japan.

Both ships sailed early in May 1631, the *Charles* up the eastern shores of the British Isles, the *Henrietta Maria* along the western. Both captains, it may be said at once, earned a place in the company of arctic leaders, although not in the first rank. However, North-West Foxe is outstanding in one way: his narration of his exploits is most readable. This conceited extrovert, this not-quite gentleman, has a quaint style and gift of phrase that frequently draws a smile, a rare experience in the cold and worthy annals of the North

Foxe was out to find the North-West Passage but also to enjoy himself. He Wrote, "I was victualed compleatly for 18 Moneths; but, whether the Baker, Brewer, Butcher, and others were Masters of their Arts, or professions, or no, I know not; but this I am sure of: I had excellent fat Beefe, strong Beere, good wheaten Bread, good Iceland Ling, Butter and Cheese of the best, admirable sacke and Aqua vitae, Pease, Oat-meale, Wheat-meale, Oyle, Spice, Sugar, Fruit, and rice; with chyrurgerie, as Sirrups, lulips, condits, trechissis, antidotes, balsoms, gummes, unguents, implaisters, oyles, potions, suppositors, and purging Pils; and if I had wanted Instruments, my Chyrugion had enough."

It is typical that this seemingly light-hearted statement contains a sly dig at Captain James, who, as a perfect gentleman, had paid tribute to his baker and cook as masters of their arts.

Foxe could be spiteful to rivals and to other people who did not please him. He chose the crew, but the master and mate were provided for him with the ship by Trinity House. He thought little of the mate, who is indifferently named Yurin or Hurin; but about the master, who is never named at all, he is clear enough: he was "the most arrogant bull calf that ever went or came as Master and the most faint-heartedest man".

That is straightforward enough, and the sequence of the voyage appears to justify it, but it is not Foxe at his best. He most attracts when he gives a quaint twist to ordinary log-keeping records. For instance: "This fulsome ugly morning presented the foulest chilhe that the whole voyage brought forth".

He is precise in his records, yet his playfulness of phrase comes out the more effectively because it is in contrast to precision. "This morning Aurora blusht, as though shee had ushered her Master from some unchast lodging, and the ayre so silent as though all those handmaides had promised secrecy." From that he continues, "The Eastermost of Mill Ile bore S.E. by E., the North Mayne from the King's Promotory, stretching E. away . . . ."

He calls the Northern Lights "Pettiedancers" and (obscurely) "henbanes". And, with the superstition of the Elizabethan heritage, he describes them not with admiration but as "most fearful to behold".

Having found Hudson Strait and passed through it, Foxe was defeated in his first attempt to get further north. So he skirted the south coast of Southampton Island and found the wide, deep sound that separates that island from the mainland. This seemed to him to offer the likeliest route, and he named it Sir Thomas Roe's Welcome. He then turned south along the western shore of Hudson Bay, already partly explored by Button and Munk.

At the end of August the *Charles* and *Henrietta Maria* met near the southern end of the bay. The behaviour of the two captains is interesting. James sent a boat with four rowers and a lieutenant to invite Foxe, his master and mate to dinner. Foxe entertained the lieutenant in his cabin, questioning him closely about James's achievements and plans, and instructed his mariners to do the same with the rowers in their mess.

The dinner that took place next day aboard the *Henrietta Maria* lasted from afternoon until next morning, "and this 17 houres was the worst spent of any time of my discoverie", says Foxe ungraciously. He grants that they were feasted by James "with varitie of such cheere as his sea provisions could afford", but "the ship . . . threw in so much water as wee could not have wanted sause if we had had roast Mutton".

He criticized his host for flying a flag, to which James answered that it was his duty, since he was bearing royal communication to the emperor of Japan. Foxe said, "Keepe it up then, but you are out of the way to Iapon, for this is not it."

James might have asked his guest what, in that case, he was doing in that part of the bay; but James was strictly polite. His own account of the meeting is brief and in no way derogatory.

Poor James cannot have been in the mood for entertaining, for he had just suffered an accident similar to Hudson's when the capstan spun in reverse. Several of the crew had been hurt and the gunner had had to have a leg amputated "at the gartering place". That operation without anaesthetic and with the ship pitching as Foxe described must have been a terrible experience. "After which we comforted each other as well as we could", wrote James.

When the ships parted, they both sighted and named the cape that forms the western lip of James Bay. It is still Cape Henrietta Maria on the map, but Foxe called it Wolstenholmes Ultimum Vale, because, he says, "I do beleeve Sir John Wolstenholme will not lay out any monies in search of this Bay."

After argument with the master, who "as usual desired to do nothing but remain in harbour", Foxe turned north and made a deep penetration into the unknown waters, now called Foxe Channel, between Southampton Island and Baffin Island. A number of his men were down with sickness, perhaps early symptoms of scurvy, but he was having no trouble from ice and was sailing fast. He was in fact heading for a narrow waterway leading deviously to the Arctic Ocean and thence to the Pacific. It cannot be called a Passage, for no ship could get through it, but it would have been a great discovery if made then instead of two centuries later.

Suddenly the *Charles* was turned about at a place that the leader named, with typical panache, Foxe his Farthest. The only explanation he gives, and not in that direct context, is that he did not feel justified in wintering and thereby expending wages and provisions for another twelve months—which is scarcely adequate. The master's journal breaks off the day before. Every expedition has its private life.

Foxe sailed home short-handed, but at the end of October he was able to record, "The 31, blessed be Almighty God, I came into the Downes with all my men recovered and sound, not having lost one Man, nor Boy, nor any manner of Tackling, having beene forth neere 6 moneths, all Glory be to God."

This in itself was a great achievement. Foxe, for all his apparent frivolity, was an effective commander. He was also an imaginative explorer with a sure sense of the likeliest lines of inquiry. He achieved more in his particular area than anyone before him (except Baffin) or for a long time after. His map was good. His book was variously received. It contained not only an account of his own voyage but also the first history of northern exploration. He was paid not a penny for his work as an explorer, only his expenses, which according to a document found in the Public Record Office amounted to £160 14s 6d. And of course he was totally engaged, when one counts the preparation and winding up, for a great deal longer than the six months of the voyage. He was an amateur adventurer, driven throughout his life (he died in 1635) by boyhood-born ambition or ideal. It is not too much to remember him by the name he gave himself, North-West Foxe.

There is no record of what, if anything, Captain James earned for his work as an explorer, but he was less fortunate in his experiences. He survived them because, unlike Foxe, he was so polite and considerate to his officers and mariners that they would do anything for him.

When Foxe turned north, James sailed southward into the bay that bears his name. From ignorance, owing to the still-persistent errors in longitude, he did not realize that this was where Hudson had been for too long, and he explored carefully. He had already decided to winter, but could not find a suitable place. Thus began what Sir John Barrow described as a "book of lamentation and weeping and great mourning". Certainly this good man suffered like Job, but his sufferings deserve record as the experiences of an early English wintering with a loyal crew. He was not actually in the Arctic. Charlton Island, where he hibernated, is in the same latitude as Oxfordshire. But the continental climate caused arctic conditions, and we are told that "All our sacke, Vineger, Oyle, and everything else that was liquid, was frozen as hard as a piece of wood, and we must cut it with a hatchet."

They searched for a sheltered cove or river mouth. They landed and made unsuccessful hunting expeditions. By November some of the crew were already sick. Captain James records: "The 19 our gunner (who as you may remember had his legge cut offe) did languish unrecoverably, and now grew very weake, desiring that, for the little time he had to live, hee might drinke Sacke altogether, which I ordered hee should doe.

"The 22, in the morning, he dyed; an honest and a strong-hearted man. Hee had a close-boorded Cabbin in the Gunroome, which was very close indeed, and as many clothes on him as was convenient 'for we wanted no clothes), and a panne with coales a fire continually in his Cabbin. For all which warmth, his playster would freeze at his wound, and his bottle of Sacke at his head. We committed him at a good distance from the Ship unto the Sea."

Before the sea became frozen all over, they suffered a terrible storm. Ice floes borne by the waves charged the anchored ship, battering her sides and sweeping away the rudder. James took desperate measures: "I went down into the hold with the carpenter, and tooke his auger and bored a hole in the ship, and let in the water."

The rest of the crew, who had been sent ashore, stood watching in the icy wind while their vessel went slowly down to settle on the shallow bottom. Then the captain joined them, and comforted them thus: "My Masters and faithfull Companions, be not dismaide for any of these disasters, but let us put our whole trust in God. . . . If it be our fortunes to end our dayes here, we are as neere heaven as in *England*; and we are much bound to God Almighty for giving us so large a time of repentance . . . ."

They built huts, and transported what they could from the ice-filled hold. It seems that they salvaged enough for subsistence, but they were no good at hunting and they were very uncomfortable, both in body and in mind. Although they insulated the huts that the carpenter built, with piled-up logs "it froze hard within a yard of the fires side".

The surgeon shaved them all, because their beards and moustaches only gathered frost; and they were at great pains to dig a well, because "melted snow-water is very unwholesome either to drinke or to dresse our victualls. It made us so short-breathed that we were scarce able to speake."

The roles of barber and surgeon were interchangeable, and Elizabethan superstition still ruled. But the courage and determination of the whole company was remarkable. "Wee then settled our bedding and provisions, providing to keepe Christmas day holy, which we solomnized in the joyfullest manner we could."

Believing that the ship was burst asunder by the swelling ice that filled her, the carpenter set about building a pinnace to get them home. The crew backed him up. Captain James had nothing but praise for them. By February two-thirds of the men were under the surgeon's care. Probably the causes were frostbite or scurvy in one of its early forms. (They had been living on flour and beef in brine.) "And yet, neverthelesse, they must worke daily, and goe abroad to fetch wood and timber, notwithstanding the most of them had no shooes to put on. Their shooes, upon coming to the fire, out of the snow, were burnt and schorcht upon their feete."

In April, working on the lump of ice that had been their ship, they came upon a cask. Two days later they chipped it out "and found it was full of very good Beere, which did much rejoyce us all, especially our sicke men, notwithstanding that it did taste a little of bulge-water".

Winter continued into what in England would have been spring, even summer. The carpenter resumed work on the pinnace, and stolidly, steadily progressed in its construction while the rest of the men mined for provisions in the sunken ship.

Captain James, persistent, modest and appreciative of small mercies, wrote, "By the 9 [May] we were come to, and got up, our five barrels of Beef and Porke, and had found 4 Buts of Beere, and one of Cyder, which God had preserved for us.

It has layne under water all winter, yet we could not perceive that it was anything the worse. God make us ever thankfull for the comfort it gave us."

A week later, "I manured a little patch of ground that was bare of snow, and sowed it with Peason [a species of pea or vetch], hoping to have some of the herbs of them shortly to eat, for as yet we can finde no greene thing to comfort us."

Hopes were high. The pinnace, "a well-proportioned vessel" big enough to take them all home, was nearing completion. Then the carpenter died—"a man generally bemoaned by us all, as much for his innate goodnesse as for the present necessity we had of a man of his quality". On the evening of his burial on land, the corpse of the gunner, buried at sea and at some distance six months previously, appeared at the ship's side, shrouded in ice. "He was as free from noysomnesse as when he was first committed to the sea. This alteration had the Ice and water and time onely wrought on him: that his flesh would slip up and downe upon his bones like a glove on a man's hand."

The gunner was chipped out and burried with "the others" (it is not exactly stated how many had died). It must have been difficult to dig graves in ground frozen within inches of the surface.

In June there was still ice about the ship, but on land there were "vetches" growing. These green things changed prospects dramatically, "For now our feeble sicke men, that could not for their lives stirre these two or three months, can indure the ayre and walke about the house; our other sicke men gather strength also, and it is wonderfull to see how soone they were recovered. We used them in this manner: Twice a day we went to gather the herbe or leafe of these Vetches, as they first appeared out of the ground; then did we wash and boyle them and so, with Oyle and Vineger that had been frozen, we did eate them. It was an excellent sustenance and refreshing; the most part of us ate nothing else. We would likewise bruise them, and take the Juyce of them, and mixe that with our drinke. We would eate them raw also with our bread."

They plugged their ship, pumped her dry and refloated her. She was sound! They sailed home—but not by the most direct route. They half circled the western coast of Hudson Bay, the wall that blocked the way to the Pacific, and which had been examined throughout most of its extent twice or thrice before. They were determined to find a passage, but there was none. So James came home without much discovery to report.

He did not appreciate his most interesting find. On 2 July, when he set sail, the wind being against him, he stood over to nearby Danby Island to gather wood for fuel. He writes, "I found two stakes driven into the ground about a foote and a half, and firebrands where a fire had beene made by them. I puld up the stakes, which were about the bignesse of my arme, and they had been cut sharpe at the ends with a hatchet, or some other good Iron toole, and driven in, as it were with the head of it. They were distant about a stones-throw from the waterside. I could not conceive to what purpose they had been there set, unlesse it were for some marke for boats. This did augment my desire to speake with the Savages; for, without doubt, they could have given notice of some Christians with whom they had some commerce."

It is most unlikely that this was the work of Eskimos or Indians. James had seen no sign of either during his wintering. Nor did they possess good iron tools with which to sharpen stakes to a pencil point. There is no record of any white pioneers reaching the shores of Hudson Bay from the south until some thirty years later, and, in any case, Danby Island is twenty miles from the shore.

So who planted those stakes, and why? James did not consider Hudson, because he believed he had wintered further to the westward; but, working on all the available evidence, with modern longitudes, it seems probable that Hudson was set adrift within a score of miles of Danby Island. It is very possible that the shallop went there with the sick men. It is logical that the fit among them would build a hut. We know from Prickett's record that Staffe went down for his box of carpenter's tools before boarding the shallop. It is not impossible that if he built a hut in 1611 some part of it was still standing in 1632.

This is little more than conjecture, but it makes the fate of those murdered men appear less forlorn and is a thread to link one expedition with another.

Chapter 13

The Incidental Benefits

Attempts to sail through the North-West Passage ended for the century in 1631. That was the finish of what has been loosely called the Elizabethan era of exploration. Eras must always be considered as elastic, not precisely defined by the mortality of monarchs; and, had the voyages just described followed the lead of Baffin instead of that of Hudson and Button, it is theoretically possible that—given amazingly ice-free seasons and the right choice taken at every turning of the maze that starts at Lancaster Sound—expeditions of the same spirit and type might have threaded the whole Passage before the Civil War. As was said at the beginning of the previous chapter, the opportunities for exploration were ideal.

But the direct objective changed. The Civil War put an end to peace and placed a tombstone, solid and simple, on the Elizabethan era as a whole. When brother ceased to be preoccupied with killing brother, a new era was born. Yet the romance of the North-West Passage was not dead. From the first it had inspired English exploration. By now the phrase alone had become evocative. Mention it and men sat up in Parliament, coffee house or tavern. The possibility of the Passage was likely to be discussed in practical terms, but the truth is that the very idea seduced like wine.

In practical terms the search had already provided certain benefits and suggested more. The north-west had not yet produced as much as the north and north-east, but that was from lack of exploitation. The Arctic contained riches—quite apart from Elizabethan dreams of gold. It was a largely untapped source and nobody doubted the right to exploit this to the full—to the extinction of the animal inhabitants. At the Creation man was given by God domination over every living thing that moveth upon the face of the earth; and, by God, he profited from it as soon as exploration showed him where to go. The walrus, whose formidable tusks curved downwards because they had been evolved for nothing more aggressive than scraping up molluscs, was slaughtered with little trouble and no danger. The lanced whale spouted his blood. Whales meant corsets more comfortable than the former straitjackets of wood and steel. They meant soap, which was in great demand, at least for washing clothes. They meant cosmetics, and fuel for lamps. They were offshore oil. Whales meant wealth. And the north-western explorers had reported many whales, in an area far distant from the over-exploited Spitsbergen waters.

This was a practical argument to back the ideal, and all argument aimed at being practical. Restoration Britain was deeply concerned with the economic position. Charles II, his Parliament and seriously-minded subjects felt that the infant Empire ought to be able not only to produce the raw materials necessary for its manufactures and transport, but also to export—to create a favourable balance of trade.

In the search for imperial wealth, eyes turned across the north Atlantic—or, rather, they remained in that direction, as they had since the days of John Cabot. Britain had colonies in North America. So had France, in the estuary of the St Lawrence (discovered by Jacques Cartier a century earlier), and the Dutch, in the Hudson river, which had been discovered for them by an Englishman. The colonies were intended for agriculture, which is slow to show a profit, particularly when forests must be cleared. They sent few worthwhile cargoes to the mother country. In fact they needed money themselves for their development. There was some trapping of fur animals, but trapping goes ill with agriculture. New England did not provide what Old England needed.

Meanwhile Fate was working out a remarkable interplay of characters and circumstances. In 1664 Colonel George Cartwright and Sir Robert Car were sent out to New England to adjudicate on colonial boundaries and, in general, to show the Restoration flag. The Commission was not conspicuously successful in establishing good relations with the Puritans, for Cartwright was believed to be a Papist and Car to have involved himself with a "naughty woman". Consequently the report that was submitted for the king's attention on Cartwright's return to England was not enthusiastic; but it concluded with the following sentence:

"Hearing also some Frenchmen discourse in New England of a passage from the West Sea to the South Sea, and of a great trade of beaver in that passage, and afterwards meeting with sufficient proof of the truth of what they had said, and knowing what great endeavours have been made for the finding out of a north-west passage, he thought them the best present he could possibly make His Majesty, and persuaded them to come to England."

Beaver was the most easily marketable fur, for it satisfied the Feltmakers, who had formed a leading City company. The North-West Passage stirred the imagination. Thus money went hand in hand with romance. The two Frenchmen referred to would have been sure of arousing interest in any case, but their striking appearance and personalities, and the story of their adventurous lives, added considerably to the impact of their arrival.

Médard Chouart, Sieur des Groseilliers—of the Gooseberry-bushes—had emigrated from France to the St Lawrence colony as a young man in about 1641. His first employment was in some non-clerical capacity with the Jesuit mission in the backwoods area known as Huronia. Unlike the New English Puritans, who would have nothing to do with the heathen savages, the Jesuits of New France pressed deeper and deeper into this land of forests, rivers and lakes, exploring, proselytizing, annexing. Not only did they learn the language of the Indian tribes and establish good relations with them, but, in addition, they claimed vast areas for France, that the native people might be brought to Christianity. Their aim was a frank combination of the spiritual and temporal. As the Spaniards had conquered with the Sword and Cross, the French missionaries set up the symbol of the Cross and fleur-de-lys. This was done without bloodshed, but not without casualties on the side of the Christian pioneers.

Flotillas of canoes passed up and down the dangerous river roads between the Great Lakes and Quebec. In 1646 news of exploration was contained in a letter written by Mère Marie of the Ursuline nuns of New France (quoted here in the translation given by Grace Lee Nute in *Caesars of the Wilderness*).

"The letters we have received from Huronia tell us that a new country has been discovered and the gateway to it is found. It is the land of the people of the sea, called in Indian Winnebago. This will be a fine mission, whither we hope to expand profitably, because these people are numerous and sedentary. The fathers are even planning to voyage on a great sea that is beyond that of the Hurons, by which they claim to find the way to China. By means of this sea, which is freshwater, they hope to discover many countries both on its shores and inland."

Thus the French dream of a North-West Passage was by a freshwater sea—as far from logical reasoning, one would have thought, as the contemporary British dream of reaching Cathay by the land- and ice-locked sea of Hudson Bay, or the Bay of the North, as it was then often called. But, in the immediate context, it was in such exploration that Groseilliers obtained his early training. He was, we are told, "a man capable of anything, bold, hardy, stubborn in his undertakings", and he had been at pains to learn the languages of the tribes.

The man with whom he eventually came to England, Pierre Esprit Radisson, was his brother-in-law and his junior by some years. Both men lived (or rather, were based) at Trois Rivières, the palisaded settlement on the St Lawrence between Quebec and Montreal. Radisson lacked the matured experience of Groseilliers, but had had as hard and adventurous a life.

While still scarcely more than a boy, he had gone duck shooting with two companions. They were surprised by Iroquois Indians. Radisson's two companions were killed but the youth himself was spared, and adopted by a family of the tribe. Radisson, as his later writings and behaviour show, was a lively extrovert, very sure of himself. His character must have intrigued his captors as much as his agility, strength and fearlessness impressed them. He learned their language, imbued himself with their psychology and copied their customs and dress—or undress. He wore feathers. He joined in the Indians' hunting expeditions.

In one such party there was another adopted captive, an Algonquian. This man persuaded Radisson to join him in murdering the rest of the party while they slept, and then making a dash for freedom. After a fortnight of hard travel they reached the St Lawrence opposite Trois Rivières; but while crossing the river they were recaptured. The Algonquian (luckily for him) was killed, and Radisson was automatically condemned to death by torture.

The Indians were connoisseurs of torture. Preliminaries, while the victim awaited his turn on the scaffold, were the pulling out of a finger nail, the thrusting of a thumb into a burning pipe bowl, and, in Radisson's case, an attempt by a four-year-old child, encouraged by its indulgent mother, to cut off one of his fingers with a sharp flint. Radisson's foster-parents saved him from death, but he had to suffer fire and red-hot iron before he was released.

By the following spring he was both recovered and forgiven. He went on the warpath with the braves in the area of the upper Hudson river. Still in his teens, he shared the ruthless life of what Rousseau called the Noble Savage; but he ended the barbarous excursion by successfully escaping to the Dutch fort of Orange, now Albany. He was sent downriver to New Amsterdam (soon to be renamed New York) and from there sailed to Holland. He went on to France and then returned to the St Lawrence. He later made a two-year journey with the Jesuits, and returned again to Trois Rivières. There he teamed up with his brother-in-law. He and Groseilliers made the most experienced, resourceful and determined partnership in the country. New France had need of such men, although the government of the colony did not appear to realize it.

New England, the New Netherlands and New France all based their economy and way of life on agriculture, as did the mother countries. All, of necessity, got a cash crop out of pelts, chiefly beaver. New England and the New Netherlands were limited in their resources, but New France had the greatest fur forest in the world stretching from its borders. However, it too suffered from restrictions, imposed partly by its own government and partly from outside.

The colony was small: in terms of the area populated by whites, a few towns and patches of land along the lower St Lawrence (Canada is a native word meaning "village"). The agriculturalist community obtained the furs almost exclusively by trade with the Indians, who brought them down to the St Lawrence by canoe. But, to keep the colony solvent, a 25 per cent tax was imposed on the pelts before export to France. That discouraged initiative; and worse followed. In the late 1640s the fierce Iroquois waged ruthless war on the Hurons of Ottawa, who, as middlemen, had collected and delivered the pelts. The Iroquois closely encircled the colony, depopulating the lower Great Lakes. In 1652-3 not one beaver skin reached Montreal.

The situation improved little during the remainder of the decade. The need, clearly, was for white traders to break through the encircling ring of Iroquois and deal direct with the hidden tribes who caught the beavers. But to do this required a licence from the governor, and it appears that graft was necessary to secure one.

Groseilliers and Radisson set off without a licence, and were absent for two years. Where exactly they went is not known, and, from what they later said and Radisson wrote, it is impossible to tell what they learned by personal exploration and what from hearsay. But they certainly dealt with the Crees, who were the master hunters in the true beaver country of the north. They found out that the Nelson river flows from Lake Winnipeg into Hudson Bay. They learned a lot about the numerous other waterways that, by portage routes, connect the Bay of the North with the St Lawrence. They returned in 1660 leading a fleet of sixty Indian canoes laden with beaver skins.

The colourful Radisson described the reaction of the factors: "In which country have you been? From whence doe you come? For wee never saw the like. From whence did come such excellent castors? Since your arrival is come into our magazine very near 600,000 pounds Tournois of that filthy merchandize, which will be prized like gold in France, and these were the very words they said to me."

Mère Marie wrote, "God has sent to the merchants more than 140,000 livres of beavers . . . . This heavenly manna has come just as those gentlemen were about to leave the country, believing that nothing further could be done for its trade."

The governor taxed and fined the two voyageurs until very little of their fortune remained. He even imprisoned them for a while for trading without a licence.

Groseilliers was proud and obstinate, and by nature litigious. His brief periods at Trois Rivières are clearly documented, because he invariably had a lawsuit when at home. He went to France to obtain redress.

He received only soft answers—which did not turn away his wrath.

Determined as ever, he went on to the French colony in Cádiz. There he won the promise of a bark to pick him up with his party and stores at Isle Percée, near the southern lip of the St Lawrence estuary—for he was determined to break the monopoly of Quebec and trade on his own. He hurried back to New France to make his preparations.

But the bark never arrived, only a little vessel much too small for his purpose, and he was told by a Jesuit that he would be punished for his plot to ruin the colony. (It may be noted that the Jesuits soon after made two attempts to reach Hudson Bay by the river route.) Groseilliers and Radisson were bitterly disappointed. Groseilliers, the master-mind, very soon decided what to do. He went to New England. The Yankees might still be lacking in exploratory initiative, but not in acumen, and the proposition submitted to them was commercially sound. As things stood, trade with the fur forest depended on canoes. Leaving aside bureaucratic and perhaps venial restrictions, this meant that trade goods could be carried inland only in small quantities and that only light cargoes could be taken out. Groseilliers suggested that, instead of being an inland town on the St Lawrence, the entrepot should be a seaport on Hudson Bay, easily accessible to the Indian hunters and suitable for ocean-going ships. The resources of the forest were infinite. Increase the carrying capacity and the trade might be multiplied a hundredfold.

The New Englanders accepted the proposition in principle but could not be induced to move quickly. Groseilliers and Radisson spent nearly three years in Boston. They were eventually provided with a ship, but she sailed late in the season and her captain's experience was of bringing sugar from Barbados. When he sighted icebergs he was dismayed to find that they were not, in Radisson's phrase, "mountains of sugar candy". He turned back.

In Boston again, waiting for another ship, Groseilliers and Radisson met Colonel George Cartwright, who took them to England—not without incident. Their ship was captured by a Dutch vessel after two hours of fighting. Cartwright's secret papers and maps of the colonies were (fortunately) thrown overboard, and the captives were put ashore in Spain.

They reached London in the plague year, 1665. Town and City had been deserted by most people who could escape to the country, but the Duke of Albemarle, who from the first was interested in Groseilliers's project, was there, as was Samuel Pepys, who later preserved Radisson's manuscripts. Robert Boyle, of the young Royal Society of London for Improving Natural Knowledge, assisted the two voyageurs to reach Oxford, where the court then was. Charles II granted them an audience, spoke with them in their own language and was clearly intrigued by their story. He asked for a written description of the country (this was perhaps the inspiration of Radisson's *Reminiscences*) and gave the two men lodging and a small allowance for living expenses. When the plague was burnt out, the voyageurs moved with the court to Windsor and thence to London.

Groseilliers's project, although delayed by many disappointments and finally thwarted in New England, had the best possible auspices in the Old Country. The king, his brother James, Duke of York, and Prince Rupert were keenly interested. So were men capable of giving practical assistance. The latest generation of merchant adventurers were more than City magnates or country gentlemen, dilettanti of cosmography. They bore noble titles, held high office and were associated with the court.

It is fascinating to picture the two voyageurs in this entourage. The Restoration beaux had no inhibitions about dress, either in colour or in cut. They out-peacocked the women. The boldest and most extravagant lady of today might be daunted by their hats. The two *coureurs de bois* were no doubt picturesque enough, but in a quite different way. They stood out, attracted attention. There would be no difficulty about communication, for all educated Englishmen spoke French—although they invariably called Groseilliers Mr Gooseberry, even in official documents.

The Frenchmen's conversation must have been a stimulating change from court gossip. Groseilliers comes down to us as bluff, truculent and probably taciturn, except when expounding his great idea. But Esprit Radisson, judging by his *Reminiscences*, was a talker (no less entertaining for being boastful) and something of an amoral poet in point of view. In his descriptions we are reminded of *Hiawatha*: "The forest primeval, the murmuring pines and the hemlock." He had enjoyed his life with the Indians, as an Indian. Like them, he compared men and animals directly, as fellow creatures, without any soul-bar. The Iroquois were owls who could see better in the night than in the day. The Huron enemy—"All those beasts gathers together againe frightened. Seeing no way of escape, got themselves all in a heaps like unto ducks that sees the eagle come to them."

His translator (he must have had his manuscript immediately translated, for effect when effect was most wanted) had little sense of grammar; but Radisson in his own language must have been a compelling talker. He was in no way squeamish about the massacres and the tortures. He seems to have enjoyed them as much as the capture of slave girls and the feastings, the award of heads for prowess. The only hint of Christian morality comes in the smug statement, "Friends, I must confesse I loved those poore people entirely well." Surely he returned to the other life only in the hope of something better—and it would have to be considerably better.

He soon had London society talking about him. His "brother" (he always used the Indian term for his partner) talked business with Sir Peter Collerton, who had been put in charge of them. Collerton was professionally concerned in righting the imperial economy. A powerful group gathered about them: the Duke of Albemarle (already mentioned); Anthony Ashley Cooper, who became the first

Earl of Shaftesbury; Sir John Collerton, Sir Peter's brother; Lord Arlington; and Lord John Berkeley. Less directly concerned, except in the early stages, was Sir George Carteret, who was reputedly the richest man in England.

It is not surprising that men with national prosperity at heart should have been interested in Groseilliers's project. It was difficult to fault it as a business proposition, almost on the scale of the East India trade. From virgin country it should bring rich cargoes to England, a raw material ideal for felting and therefore for home manufacture and export. Incidentally, it would do down the French, whose Canadian colony was at best a nuisance. And it sounded a good personal investment.

However, it is surprising and most interesting that Groseilliers's commercial proposition took second place to the hope it gave of realizing the dream of the North-West Passage. Men of science were attracted by that aspect. The Secretary of the Royal Society wrote to Robert Boyle expressing his "great joy at ye discovery of a North-west-passage". He had heard, he said, that these men "went out of a Lake in Canada, into a river, which discharged itself North-west into the South-Sea, into which they went, and returned North-East into Hudson's Bay". He asked for confirmation. There is no record of Boyle's answer.

The financial backers of the voyage eventually launched had the same point in the forefront of their minds. Their instructions to the captains included, "You are to have in yor thoughts the discovery of the Passage into the South sea and to attempt it as occasion shall offer with the advice and direction of Mr. Gooseberry and Mr. Raddison, or one of them, they having told us that it is but 7 daies padling or sailing from the River where they intend to trade and Harbour unto the stinking Lake and not above 7 daies more to the streight wch leads into the sea they call the South sea and thence but forty or fifty leagues to the sea it selfe, in all wch streight it Ebbs and flowes by meanes whereof the passage up and downe will be quicke, and if it be possible you are to gett so much light in this matter before the returne of the *Nonsuch* Ketch as may encourage us the next spring to send a vessell on purpose for that discovery."

The stream of interest in the North-West Passage had been flowing underground since Captain James's unhappy expedition of 1630–1. Cromwell never thought of it, and his ferocious repression of Ireland did not produce another Gilbert or Frobisher. But, as soon as it reached soil that allowed it to break free, it burst out as powerful as ever, sweeping away logical considerations. The instructions just quoted must have been well considered, but even allowing for the limits of contemporary knowledge they make a nonsense of North American geography. The "stinking Lake" may have been Winnipeg or the Green Bay of Michigan, but how could anyone paddle to either in seven days from Hudson Bay? Even then the breadth of the continent was beginning to be comprehended. Drake, for one, had been on the other side of it a century before. How could anyone hope to cross it by canoe in two or three weeks? Topographically, if a river flowed from the stinking lake to Hudson Bay, could another flow from it to the Pacific? And, if there did exist a waterway right across the continent, would it not be salt or at least brackish? The Royal Society was surely being less than scientific. But that is one of the glorious things about the North-West Passage. It existed in men's minds as something above natural laws, commercial rules, navigational facts, commonsense, logic. It was nearer to an article of religious faith.

Yet the voyage to Hudson Bay was most carefully prepared, every practical detail considered; and commercially it was viable, as it proved. But before describing it let us us examine Groseilliers's motive. Surely it was simple enough. He felt that he had been cheated by the governor of New France out of a fortune won—for the benefit of the colony as well as himself—by two years of stress, danger and enterprise. He went to his mother country for redress. The ministers of Louis XIV politely shrugged their shoulders. (We may spare a thought as to what might have happened if France had given Groseilliers a ship and thus enabled him to develop the great Canada we now know from Hudson Bay.) Groseilliers was snubbed, and looked for patronage from another country.

In this he followed the precedent of Columbus and Magellan; but he had no grand ideas of worldwide discovery. Sebastian Cabot is a better comparison. Groseilliers wanted to earn money in the life he knew and loved. It was England that made him appear an idealist. It is doubtful whether he even mentioned the North-West Passage before he met Cartwright in Boston, and then it may have been in answer to a typically English question. In England he found that it was the North-West Passage that sparked the fire, and so he played on it. He cared nothing for England, nor did Radisson. Their loyalty to this country depended on nothing more than a grudge against their own. And it is scarcely likely that a *coureur de bois* would want to find a way to China.

It is difficult to judge fairly to what extent Groseilliers and Radisson were responsible for the rumour, almost the certainty, that the North-West Passage was as good as found. They of all people must have known that there was no way for canoes, let alone ships, through the continent. They had either travelled from one of the Great Lakes to Hudson Bay or they had not. If they had not, they lied in any positive statement about a passage. If they had made the journey, they lied if they said it was navigable in a nautical sense, meaning without portages. Of the vast expanse westward of the lakes their knowledge must have been almost entirely hearsay. So, if they did in fact speak of a passage to the South Sea, they used an unjustified factual inexactitude. At this safe distance of time we are attracted by their personalities, but cannot put much trust in their word.

Yet they were trusted at the time. For three years they were kept comfortably and consulted on every aspect of the proposed voyage, such as the trade goods required: brandy, because the French had used this fire water for barter; tobacco from Virginia; and wampum, which was shells found principally in Long Island. Thus they were partly occupied (and Radisson wrote his *Reminiscences*) while the long delay continued. Partly this was owing to the fact that the Dutch at that time commanded the Channel, and they and the French were alert for any expedition bound for the North-West. Principally it was owing to the casual, gentlemen's agreement between the backers: no individual ventured more than he would lightheartedly have done on a game of cards. There was talk of a royal charter, but no document can be found to support this. Accounts were kept in the most haphazard manner. A totally unsuitable ship was bought, and had to be sold again. Groseilliers and Radisson, men of action, must have been driven almost out of their wits by inaction.

At long last, on 5 June 1668, the *Eaglet* and the *Nonsuch* sailed from the Thames. The *Eaglet*, one of the "small vessels" of the Royal Navy, lent by the king, carried Radisson. Groseilliers was on the forty-four ton *Nonsuch* ketch, which was captained by Zachariah Gillam, a New Englander who had been a junior officer on the sugar-candy trip five years earlier.

So far as the vessels were concerned, this was not intended as an exploratory voyage. The ships were to carry the men to a particular place where the inland explorations, and trading, were to begin. In this respect it is entirely different from anything previously described.

The king's ship lost her mast in mid-Atlantic and had to turn back—with the unfortunate Radisson. "Old Zach" Gillam (he gained a New England reputation and nickname) carried on into Hudson Bay.

Having reached this vast expanse of water from a point that he had never seen (if, indeed, he had seen the bay at all), Groseilliers may be excused for being confused. The only river that might conceivably lead to the Pacific from Hudson Bay is the Nelson, which comes from Lake Winnipeg, into which the Saskatchewan river flows from the west. The mouth of the Nelson is in the middle of the western shore. Groseilliers guided Gillam (we must suppose he did the guiding) down the eastern shore, much as Hudson had gone. They ended up in the estuary of the Rupert river, near the bottom of James Bay, and within a day's sailing of Captain James's winter quarters and the probable whereabouts of Hudson's death.

In a little ceremony before an audience of silent trees, the ship's company took possession of the territory in the name of King Charles, and they built Fort Charles. This, the first of a generation of forts that staked out a period of British imperial expansion, deserves description.

The report of Captain Gillam's evidence to the Royal Society (we may imagine those learned gentlemen listening to it) stated, "When they came a shore, they built ymselves a house of wood, and dugg a cellar 12 foot deep into ye ground, where they putt some barrels of good bier, wch at their time of coming away being taken out, after it had layn there 8 or 9 months prov'd very excellent liquor; they in ye mean time brewing all the winter long of provision of malt, they had taken with yem."

From other references it is apparent that the place was a fort in name only—at this stage at least—the defences being only against discomfort. A two-storey building rose above the cellar, the outer walls being formed of logs caulked with moss. On the ground floor were the kitchen, dining room and sleeping quarters, and a wood fire was kept blazing. Above this was the store for biscuits, flour, peas and oatmeal. Barrelled beef, pork and butter, and the beer brewed for everyday use were kept in the cellar. Outside there was a separate bakehouse, where venison pastry was made.

There was no repetition of the ordeal suffered by the crew of the *Henrietta Maria*, but there is no mention of exploration. In April, when the trapping season would have been ending, the Indians began to visit the party. A total of 300 visitors is given—a large number in that lonely place where Hudson had seen only one native, and James none.

In late summer the ship sailed home. The *London Gazette* recorded her arrival at Deal: "This last night came in here the *Nonsuch* Ketch which having endeavoured to make out a passage by the North-West, was in those seas environed with Ice, which opposing her progress, the men were forced to hall her on shoar and provide against the ensuing cold of a long Winter; which ending, they returned with a considerable quantity of Beaver, which made them some recompense for their cold confinement."

This recompense amounted at a sale to £1,379 6s 10d, and one wonders if it was not the true and only purpose of the voyage. Under the guidance of Groseilliers, the North-West Passage had again become a thing of dreams.

Chapter 14

The Hudson's Bay Company

Nothing succeeds like success, and nothing is more quickly complimented by being copied. France became actively interested in a North-West Passage, as it had not been since Cartier discovered that the St Lawrence is a river, not a strait.

This interest was curiously born. Back in England with the dismasted *Eaglet*, Radisson found that the adventurers were as keen as ever on the Hudson Bay project, and off he sailed again with the same captain, Stannard, but in a different ship, the *Wivenhoe*. This second voyage was scarcely more successful than the first, but on board was a Dutchman, Lawrence van Heemskerk, who encouraged Radisson to talk—never, perhaps, a difficult thing to do—and to talk in such detail that on his return to Europe van Heemskerk was able to go to the French court with a well-formulated plan for a trading voyage to Hudson Bay. This plan can scarcely have differed from that put before Louis XIV by Groseilliers in 1660; but, as in England in the days of Cabot, so it was in seventeenth-century France. In this mysterious business of exploration the monarch was more ready to trust a foreigner, and van Heemskerk was given three ships. They failed to reach their intended destination, but the venture marked the beginning of French rivalry with Britain in Hudson Bay.

New France also was stung to action. In 1671 we find Colbert, King Louis's Minister for Commerce and Marine, writing as follows to Jean Talon, the Intendant of New France (and incidentally conveying a double interest, such as that that had swayed the English at the time of Frobisher's voyages): "Your action in sending Sieur de la Salle to the southward and Sieur de Saint Lusson to the northward to discover the passage to the South Sea is very good; but the principal thing to which you must look in these kinds of discoveries is to find copper mines . . . ."

There is much more to be said about French rivalry, which quickly became effective, but first we must record the formation of the greatest lode stream of the North-West Passage—the one that drove more power mills than any other and still drives them—the Hudson's Bay Company.

While Old Zach Gillam and the *Nonsuch* ship's company were brewing beer at Fort Charles, while Groseilliers was trading with the Indians, drawing them away from their commercial allegiance to the St Lawrence French, and while Radisson was talking injudiciously to van Heemskerk, the group of adventurers who had launched the *Nonsuch* voyage on a loose-knit gentlemen's agreement were forging themselves into a businesslike organization with City as well as court backing, proper accountancy and reasonably adequate capital. The fur sale after the ship's return was sufficient proof that the plan was viable. Then, to cut a not very long story to a sentence, the Hudson's Bay Company was formed by royal charter on 2 May 1670.

The East India Company, at the time a much more important organization, has long since passed away into the archives. That suggests that the Hudson's Bay Company's charter was worded with precision and in such a way as to keep its options open for the future. That is so; but one's first impression upon reading it is of arrogance. Prince Rupert, the Duke of Albemarle, the Earl of Craven, Lord Arlington, Lord Ashley (Anthony Ashley Cooper), Sir John Robinson, Sir Robert Vyner (the king's banker and money lender) and eleven other gentlemen were "formed into a body politique by the name of Governors and Adventurers trading into Hudsons Bay". They were granted "sole trade and commerce of all those Seas Straights Bayes Rivers Lakes Creeks and Sounds in whatever latitude they shall be that lie within the entrance of the Straights commonly called Hudsons Straights together with all the Lands and Territory . . . upon the Contryes and Coastes and confynes of the Seas Bayes Lakes Rivers Creekes and Soundes aforesaid that are not actually possessed by or granted to any of our Subjects or any other Christian Prince or State". Close upon these sweeping rights there comes (from the already drafted grant of October 1669) the typically English obligation to pay two elks and two black beaver whenever the king or his descendants should enter the territory.

Without going further into the niceties of the charter—and they are very nice—it is enough to say that the company could explore where it liked, do what it liked and exploit the result to the full so long as it did not tread on any Christian toes and so long as it entered the territory so widely defined via Hudson Strait. If those provisions were observed it could expand as far as the Pacific coast and China; but it had to start upon this North-West Passage by the wrong turning.

In the light of contemporary geographical knowledge this one condition was neither unpractical nor in the event unfortunate. It bound development to the continent, not to the distant channels between ice-bound islands where the only possible sea route actually lay. It allowed for a river and lake route such as Groseilliers had envisaged and claimed to know. It allowed for the continental Arctic coast to be explored, which proved of value to the Passage proper, and it encouraged the development of Canada as a whole.

The company did not mince words or minimize threats so far as its self-asserted rights were concerned. Rupert Land—in effect a colony stretching outward from the southern shores of Hudson Bay—must remain inviolate to other traders. Any such poachers would forfeit ship and merchandise and have to pay bail of £1,000 not to repeat the offence. (The legal rights were vested in London, where any case not summarily dealt with would have to be heard.) The charter was magnificently imperial and arbitrary.

It is justifiable to suspect that those reponsible for this arrogance were nonetheless in some private doubt. No attempt to have the charter ratified by Parliament was made before 1690, and even then Parliament confirmed it only for seven years. So it dragged on, far into the next century, when, Britain having conquered Canada, it was the British North-westers of Montreal who challenged it, by sending a ship to Charlton Island. But we are concerned with more immediate events, with a period during which Hudson Bay was still believed to offer a passage of some sort to the Pacific.

The company, being duly chartered under the royal seal, and under the governorship of Prince Rupert, it was necessary to find an executive governor of Rupert Land. The choice was typical of the shrewdness and unconventionality of the Merry Monarch. Charles Bayley was a long-bearded Quaker who spoke his mind at whatever cost. Seven years previously he had written to the king telling him of a whirlwind that would sweep the kingdom unless he gave up his "chambering and wantonness". He had been in trouble ever since, generally in prison.

Charles kept Bayley in the Tower for "seditious practices", paying his personal expenses—for in those days there was a private-prisoners scheme, comparable to that of our private patients. He was allowed freedom for a mission to France, and returned to prison. He was a patently good man, and competent, but a confounded nuisance to the Establishment.

Sir John Robinson, Lieutenant of the Tower, was one of the adventurers of the

Hudson's Bay Company. In an inspired moment he suggested that this tiresome prisoner might be a useful governor of Rupert Land. Bayley was offered freedom on condition that he took up this important appointment. He did, and on the whole did it well. The Passage had been involved with some strange characters, and in that association it remained.

Bayley sailed on the first voyage to Hudson Bay after the charter had been sealed. The ships were the *Wivenhoe*, captained by Newland, and the company's frigate *Prince Rupert*, under Zach Gillam. The latter vessel, with Groseilliers on board, went straight to Fort Charles, which was given some reason for its title by the emplacement of guns.

Bayley and Radisson in the *Wivenhoe* found their way to the mouth of the Nelson river. A territorial establishment there was essential to the company's plans. The Nelson offered the best nucleus for a colony, the best opportunity for trade, and the best hope—probably the only one—for a water route to the Pacific. We have already begun to suspect that the discovery of such a route was not really a prime purpose of the company, but the North-West Passage was still its marching song.

The *Wivenhoe* did not reach Port Nelson (which as yet, of course, was no more than the river mouth) without suffering storms and damage from rocks. When eventually it did arrive, Governor Bayley landed and with due ceremony took possession of "all the Landes and Territoryes . . . . for his Majesty and in token thereof nayled up the Kinges Armes in Brasse on a Small Tree". There was not even a wandering Indian to witness this important act of acquisition—and it *was* important, as was, still more, the strange disappearance of any written reference to it during the vital years that followed. Only Nature stood witness, and she reacted with a furious storm, driving the *Prince Rupert* out of the river mouth and sending her scuttling across the bay to the ill-named Cape Comfort.

The ship's company were in a bad way. Two men had died, Captain Newland was dying and several were ill. Radisson with a boat crew rowed to Fort Charles to report. Gillam went back with him and brought the *Prince Rupert* to harbour near the sheltered place found for the *Wivenhoe*.

Wigwams, stooks of sticks draped with old sails, were made for the crew, it being too late to build a house for them. Captain Newland died and was buried with full military honours. A farewell volley was fired above the heads of the trees.

> . . . the little port
> Had seldom seen a costlier funeral.

Never, in fact; it was a solemn beginning.

Given the circumstances, Bayley did well: he established friendly relations with the Indians when they came in for trade; he bought Rupert Land from them—a transaction that they cannot have understood; and he sent Groseilliers and Radisson off exploring to the Moose river and elsewhere—for trade. At Christmas, it was recorded, "wee made merry remembering our Friends in England, having for Liquor Brandy and strong beer and for Food plenty of Partridges and Venson". Brandy was also traded to the Indians. And there was (later) a recorded incident when a chief found his squaw in the Fort and expressed his disapproval by hitting her on the head with a tomahawk. Hudson Bay undoubtedly eroded Bayley's strict puritanical principles; but on one point he stood firm throughout his governorship. It had always been a standing order that crews should observe Divine Service daily. Bayley could not countenance that, and this was a point later picked on by the Jesuits (leading opponents of Britain's claims in the bay), who, although they might disapprove of the Book of Common Prayer, as did the Puritans, nonetheless condemned the lack of formal worship.

The colonists of New France saw their fur trade, their cash-crop, being cut off. Intendant Talon raised the banner of resistance. He, like the British, used the North-West Passage as a marching song. A real threat was being posed to French trade and expansion, and, had it not been that the monarchs of France and Britain had something in common—their belief (tacit or otherwise) in the Divine Right of Kings—a war, as opposed to a quarrel, might soon have followed. As it was, Louis XIV and Charles II not only had sympathy for each other, but also, to a considerable extent, depended on each other. Louis wanted Charles to declare himself a Catholic. Charles's brother James, the future king, was an ardent Jesuit. The trouble in the New World was much less important than events in Europe.

The situation is comparable to that of two families where the parents are friends, or at least want to keep on good terms, and the children quarrel. So for some time there was quarrelling and fighting, but not family war. This does not mean that the parents failed to back up their children. They reacted diplomatically to the complaints of their young ones, yet still bowed to each other in public.

The English were in a weaker position diplomatically than they might have been, for they had failed to establish a colony on the Nelson river and did not continuously maintain Fort Charles in Rupert Land. For one good reason or another, they went home for most of the winters before 1675. Meanwhile New France was becoming increasingly restive. Intendant Talon was not one to let foreign grass grow under his feet. He took steps. He despatched Father Abanel with a letter to Groseilliers and instructions that he was to persuade the Indians to return to the old manner of trade.

The Jesuit, who was described by Gillam as "a little owld man", travelled altogether some 2,500 miles, making portages round 200 waterfalls and ascending or descending 400 rapids. On the way he "had the consolation to see the glory of Jesus Christ and his flock increased by thirty-three little innocents upon whom I conferred Baptism". One cannot help wondering how much these little innocents resembled the child who had tried to cut off Radisson's finger with a flint.

Father Abanel's doctrine for the Indians, spiritual-*cum*-commercial, was summed up as follows.

" 'I love God,' says the Frenchman to you. 'I will have no allies or kinsfolk that acknowledge the Demon for their master and have recourse to him in their needs. My friendship, alliance and kinship are not to be merely on earth and in this world; I desire them to be continued in the other, after death and to be maintained in Heaven. And to this end, abandon the plan of carrying on commerce with the Europeans who are trading toward the North Sea, among whom prayer is not offered to God; and resume your old route to Lake St. John, where you will always find some black gown to instruct and baptize.' "

He was the archetypal missionary with an imperial purpose. It took him two years to find Groseilliers. How much he then swayed him is not known. He continued his tireless journeyings in an attempt to turn the loyalty of the Indians back to the St Lawrence; he tore down the British royal arms. Bayley, as governor of Rupert Land, not as a Quaker, felt compelled to take the Jesuit in charge and send him to England as a seditious element—which he himself had been considered in the past.

In England the little old man was treated with great respect (no doubt the king and the Duke of York had something to do with this) and was given financial help to continue to France. To that country Groseilliers and Radisson soon followed him, terminating any agreement they may have had with the Hudson's Bay Company and breaking their allegiance to Britain. A grudge against the mother country gives no bond of loyalty to another.

In spite of the departure of the two men who had sparked off the venture, the company established itself in the Bottom of the Bay, as James Bay was called, with forts or "factories" at the mouths of the Rupert, Moose and Albany rivers. Looking further afield, in 1675 the company obtained, at the cost of £65, a charter to develop Busse Island, which was reported to be rich in "whales easie to be struck, Sea-Horse, Seal and Codd in abundancie". It will be recalled that the existence of this island had been reported in the log of the *Busse of Bridgewater*, one of Frobisher's vessels, 103 years previously. It had then been put on the map and had remained there without clear confirmation. (Henry Hudson had looked for it without success, but Gillam claimed to have seen it several times.) The *Prince Rupert* spent a whole season in a careful search, but it was not there.

The company could ill afford that its principal ship should waste a year. The fur cargoes were fairly good, but expenses were high: there was not sufficient capital for expansion, and the committee on several occasions had to borrow. And there still was no colony on the Nelson.

Finally, in 1682 (the year when Prince Rupert died and was followed by the Duke of York as governor of the company) the company sent to the river mouth the *Prince Rupert*, commanded by Captain Zachariah Gillam and with John Bridgar (who had been appointed governor of the proposed Nelson colony) on board. After so long a delay the committee had chosen an unfortunate year, for there were two other parties in the area. One was a French expedition with as much official backing as the English, intent upon claiming and developing the Nelson area. The other consisted of fourteen young men from New England on board the *Bachelor's Delight*, all "very resolute Fellowes". They cared nothing for royal charters and proclamations to the trees. They were, quite frankly, interlopers who were there to make money.

In this story, where recorded facts are sometimes stranger than anything that would be accepted from a writer of fiction, one must picture three separate Edens within a few miles of each other but each unconscious of the others. Stranger still, the leader of the Bachelors was Benjamin Gillam, who knew nothing of his father Zachariah's movements.

Topography explains the first point. The Nelson and Hayes rivers flow into Hudson Bay within a few miles of each other, a long tongue of thickly wooded country between. Radisson and Groseilliers, who were leading the French, chose the Hayes, presumably because from their previous experience it offered better access to the interior and the Indian Trappers. There, no doubt with the usual rigmarole of proclamation and the nailing up of royal arms, they began to build a fort. Meanwhile the English were doing the same at the mouth of the Nelson. The New England Bachelors were already established on an island a few miles up the Nelson.

This record of events derives mainly from Radisson, who seems to have taken over leadership of the old partnership (he was much younger than Groseilliers, who must then have been past the age of enterprise). Apart from various affidavits later sworn in court, he is our only source, no doubt biased.

On returning from a canoe journey to make trade contact with the inland Indians (*not* to find the North-West Passage), he heard cannon fire, and on investigation found that the explosion had been set off by the Bachelors, perhaps in a moment of enthusiasm. If so it was their last. Radisson visited their island and told them that they were poachers, for this was a part of King Louis's realm. He occupied a fort nearby, he said, with a vastly superior force and they stood to lose their freedom as well as any furs they might have gained by illicit trade. But Radisson was an old acquantance, if not a friend, of Benjamin Gillam, and he magnanimously promised him "protection".

After this moral victory Radisson paddled down the Nelson in his canoe and encountered the *Prince Rupert*—which he must have recognized. He landed; the ship anchored, then sent a boat after him. He spoke to the crew first in one of the Indian languages and then in French, neither of which they understood. Having thus established his intellectual superiority, he cocked his musket and, speaking in English, forbade them to land.

Going on board the *Prince Rupert* (he and the captain were old enemies, for, while an employee of the Hudson's Bay Company, Radisson had denounced Captain Gillam for indulging in private trading), he made the acquaintance of John Bridgar, governor of the still non-existent colony. Bridgar appears as a true English gentleman, strictly honourable and of limited intelligence. He claimed that the British had prior right to the area. Radisson, of course, knew this to be true: not only had Hudson been in the bay at the beginning of the century, with Button, Foxe and James following, but, in addition, he himself had been present at the ceremony when, at that very same place, Governor Bayley had nailed up the royal arms on a small tree. Yet he claimed it for France as contiguous with Quebec—which was the official French line.

They agreed to differ, meanwhile continuing to build their forts and do their trade. Bridgar's limit of intelligence is expressed by his acceptance of Radisson's good faith. Radisson had promised co-operation in this lonely place and casually referred to his two large ships (they were very small) at anchor within ten miles, with a third expected shortly and with a large body of men constructing a fort (actually a few men were building a log cabin). He made no mention of the New England Bachelors, keeping that as a card up his sleeve. "I was right to conceal from him and to do what I did", he remarks. "Not having men enough to come to an open struggle, it was necessary to make use of stratagem."

Fate, showing no greater sense of moral responsibility than Radisson did, drove the *Prince Rupert* out of harbour in a storm, at a time when only Captain Gillam and five men were aboard. Inadequately manned, she went down with all hands. Thus Governor Bridgar was deprived of his ship and most of his provisions, which had not yet been landed. Young Gillam was not informed of his father's death until he was at the French fort on the Hayes river, believing himself a guest but actually a prisoner. Then Radisson captured the Bachelors' camp and vessel by surprise and without bloodshed. Thus he had both rival parties in his hands.

But he did not himself remain unscathed. The spring ice, surging with the thaw, cut away his two little ships at water level. From the two vessels, his men patched together one.

Thus, with the autumn of 1683 approaching, the men still alive—for a number had died from natural causes, if scurvy can be so considered—were left with only two ships, the reconstructed one and the *Bachelors' Delight*. In the latter, Radisson and all his men (except those left behind to maintain the French colony), most of the English and all the New Englanders sailed for Quebec. The governor of the unconsummated British colony went to the Bottom of the Bay in the reconstructed French vessel, which was not fit for the open sea.

There is some poetic justice. In Quebec Radisson was charged the quarter tax on the furs, his own and those he had acquired, while the *Bachelors' Delight* and her crew were allowed to go free to New England.

Radisson went to London, where the Hudson's Bay Company gave him a gratuity of £25 for "helping" Bridgar's party and received him back into its service. He took the oath of allegiance for the second time and in 1648 returned to Nelson in the *Happy Return*. There he found his young relative Médard Chouart, Groseilliers's son, in charge of the French Canadian company that was attempting to usurp Fort York (the English fort). Chouart agreed to trade in conjunction with Radisson and accompany him to London with the full cargo of furs next season. This he did—and joined the Hudson's Bay Company.

Scarcely had they left when a French ship intercepted a small English supply vessel bound for Fort York. The French officers discussed among themselves whether they were justified in capturing it, since the two countries were not at war. They were persuaded by the Jesuit chaplain that "natural justice", the Hudson's Bay Company having taken furs that belonged by right to France, was on their side. When the English captain pointed out that the vessel belonged to him personally, and that only the cargo was the company's, he was told by the French "that the Company of England was too just to let him lose anything without compensating him".

As this Gilbertian story well illustrates, the two countries' rivalry in Canada did not at this time involve bloodshed. However, worse was to follow, and must at least be sketched, since it matters to our theme as a dam does to a river. For a quarter of a century no one thought of anything except playing French and English.

In 1688 de Troyes led a hundred men from Montreal up the Ottawa river, then across country and down the Moose river to James Bay, where he destroyed the forts and captured furs and shipping. De Troyes's own account paints a picture of a brilliant and heroic military operation. It was a magnificently achieved canoe journey culminating in an entirely unexpected terrorist attack in time of peace. The British were taken off guard, sleeping, not even a sentry on duty. Most of the personnel were workmen brought out to build the forts. They did not understand what it was all about and, in one instance, had left a ladder standing outside the palisade.

Open war followed three years later—a declaration made in Europe for purely European reasons. It made little difference to the quarrel in Hudson Bay, merely intensifying it. Ships were sunk. Forts were captured and recaptured and burned down. The French, thanks to their base on the St Lawrence, gained the ascendancy. The factory at Albany beat off an attack similar to that by de Troyes, but at one stage it was the only post that the Hudson's Bay Company retained. There was, of course, no exploration.

The third governor of the company had been Lord Churchill, the future Duke of Marlborough. Although during his governorship the company was at its lowest ebb, it was through his victories in Europe that peace at last returned to the bay, following the Treaty of Utrecht in 1713.

Chapter 15

Land and Fresh Water

We have seen that the intoxicating effect of the North-West Passage was always enhanced when there existed also the hope of expanding trade or of finding valuable minerals. In 1719 all three combined to launch another expedition.

James Knight had been a servant of the Hudson's Bay Company almost from the beginning, occasionally a trouble to the committee, for he was of independent mind and obstinate, but never lacking in enterprise and courage. He had taken a leading part in recapturing forts and factories from the French and had established Prince of Wales Fort, a new post on the Churchill river in the north.

Concerning the Northern Indians he reported to the committee, "All the knives, awls, hand-cuffs, rings bands as goes about their headgear [are] of Pure Virgin Copper as they take up out of a River . . . . But that is not still what I am Endeavouring to gett or Endeavour to discover; there is a Parcell of Indians as lyes upon the west Seas as has a Yellow Mettle as they make Use of, as these do copper."

Among his colleagues in the bay Knight was carefully secretive about his plans, but he informed the committee, of which he was a member, that he would be returning to London on completion of his contract (he must have been well over sixty). They subtly conveyed their interest by sending him eight dozen bottles of wine for the voyage.

He reached England in 1718 with samples of the copper (not the gold) and a plan that reads like the plot of a fictional treasure hunt in which awkward geographical facts are ignored. The copper-yielding river is now clearly identifiable as the Coppermine. The gold was found at the mouth of "a very Great River that comes out of the West Sea"—a term then used synonymously with the South Sea or Pacific. This may have been the Mackenzie somehow confused with a river of the Yukon or Alaska. Knight inquired of the Indians whether these rivers could be reached by sea. He was told that they could not—there was no strait. But he decided otherwise, apparently on the reported evidence that once beyond the Barren Lands the trees grew taller and taller to the north-westward, thus proving proximity to the mild West Sea. The Straits of Anian were more than a fable. Knight would sail through the North-West Passage, open up trade in a virgin area, ballast his ships with copper and bring back a cargo of gold.

Such was the magic of the mixture that the committee were persuaded. They provided two ships; but, forseeing that the old man might not survive the voyage, they instructed his second-in-command to "find out the Straights of Anian, and to make what Discoveries you possibly can, and to obtain all sorts of Trade and Commerce . . . . Especially to find out the Gold and Copper Mines if possible."

The *Albany* and the *Discovery* sailed into the north of Hudson Bay—and disappeared. For the committee this meant a dead loss of £8,000, which effectively discouraged them from further exploration. They did dispatch search vessels, but to no effect, and for a generation the mystery remained. The most popular theory was that Knight had found the Passage and sailed through it to the Pacific, there meeting some disaster.

During this period the little-known Southampton Island section of the bay was thoroughly explored by expeditions launched by the Admiralty and a private backer, Arthur Dobbs. In 1641 Captain Christopher Middleton led two ships from England and wintered in the Churchill river, his men suffering from scurvy. Middleton believed that the cure for this disease was rum punch. With the remainder of his crews he explored Roe's Welcome, the sound between Southampton Island and the mainland, and found that the Wager river was simply that. Dobbs, an Irish parliamentarian, refused to accept this: the Wager was the Passage, he insisted. He even went so far as to assert that Middleton had been bribed to falsify his log and conceal the existence of the Passage so that the Hudson's Bay Company might maintain its monopoly in the area.

Another expedition was sent out, under Captain Moore. This confirmed what Middleton had stated, but pointed at Chesterfield Inlet as likely to be the Passage. Captain Norton in 1762 proved that it was not. Thus, a century and a half after Baffin had said that Hudson Bay offered no route to westward, the fact had been accepted—at least for the moment.

Five years after Norton's voyage, a Hudson's Bay Company sloop called at Marble Island, near the mouth of Chesterfield Inlet and 400 miles north of Churchill. The young mate, Samuel Hearne, landed with a boat's crew and there found two wrecks lying in five fathoms of water, and the ruins of a house on the shore. While they were examining these things the men noticed that they were being observed with the greatest interest and excitement by a very old Eskimo. They asked him if he knew anything about their find, and he told a story that seemed to explain the disappearance of Knight's expedition.

Many years ago, he said, the two ships had entered the cove late in the season, and the larger vessel had suffered severe damage in so doing. However, the white men, at that time about fifty in number, had landed and built a house.

When the Eskimos, having wintered on the mainland, returned to Marble Island in the next open season, the white men were much reduced in number and those who remained seemed very unhealthy. But they were busily engaged, apparently in boat-building. Hearne found near the house a great quantity of oak chippings, evidently made by a carpenter's adze.

For some reason—probably failing will and the effects of scurvy and malnutrition—none of the white men managed to get away, and by winter there were only twenty still alive.

That winter the Eskimos camped on the opposite side of the cove and supplied the survivors with seal and whale meat; but in the spring they went to the mainland sixteen miles away, and when they returned in summer there were only five Englishmen still alive. These eagerly accepted raw seal meat and whale blubber and gulped it down. The effect on their empty bellies was that three of them died almost immediately. The remaining two just managed to bury them.

Let Hearne finish the account as he had it from the ancient Eskimo: "Those two survived many days after the rest, and frequently went to the top of an adjacent rock, and earnestly looked to the South and East, as if in expectation of some vessel coming to their relief. After continuing there a considerable time together, and nothing appearing in sight, they sat down close together, and wept bitterly. At length one of the two died, and the other's strength was so far exhausted, that he fell down and died also, in attempting to dig a grave for his companion. The sculls and other large bones of those two men are now lying above-ground close to the house."

Possibly this is not a complete and accurate account. The passivity of the white men is hard to accept. The Eskimos may have stolen vital tools and materials or otherwise have actively obstructed attempts to escape or to obtain relief: metal and timber were almost irresistible temptations. But the significance of this incident in this slim slice of history is that it must have helped to focus the mind of Samuel Hearne on the idea of reaching the mouth of the Coppermine river overland and by canoe. He had already caught the eye of his superiors "by his ingenuity, industry, and a wish to undertake some arduous enterprise by which mankind might be benefitted".

He suggested the journey to Moses Norton, governor of Prince of Wales Fort at Churchill, who put up the idea to the committee. They accepted it. To evaluate the proposition at the most practical level, a hand sledge, canoe and one man cost nothing compared to a couple of ships and a crew of fifty. The committee had almost all to gain in the eyes of their shareholders and no more than petty cash to lose. In the event, Hearne's journey inaugurated a new form of exploration, or, more accurately, a form that Groseilliers and Radisson had talked about and not attempted—reaching out to the Pacific by fresh water. It achieved something vitally important in the North-West Passage search. But besides that it began the development of north-west Canada in the only way practical in that land of water and portage. It helped to justify the compulsive urge by demonstrating the much wider fringe benefits.

Hearne was determined to achieve his object whatever the cost in terms of hardship and danger and even of conscience and self-respect. Except as regards such mapping as he had to do, he made himself into an Indian, using the Indians' techniques and adopting as far as possible their mentality. However, Moses Norton insisted that he should take no Indian women in his party.

He made two false starts to his search. On his first attempt, he left Churchill in November 1769 with a few "Home Guard" (Cree servants of the company) and some Northern Indians, neither group having any real interest in the journey. On the first night one of the Northern Indians deserted, leaving Hearne to drag his sledge load. Three weeks later the rest of the Indians decamped, with the provisions and stores, "making the woods ring with their laughter" and leaving Hearne to find his way back to Churchill, living precariously off the country.

He started again in February, accompanied at first only by Northern Indians. He travelled as they did, with a gun and a blanket, and of necessity adapted himself to their improvident ways. If they killed deer, some days were spent "in feasting and gluttony". They would then hurry on "without any other subsistence than a pipe of tobacco and a glass of water". Twenty miles in a day was an ordinary distance and forty-five is mentioned.

It was feast or famine. In the latter situation, he says, "I have frequently seen the Indians examine their wardrobe, which consisted chiefly of skin clothing, and consider what part could best be spared; sometimes a piece of old, half rotten deerskin, and at others a pair of old shoes, were sacrificed to alleviate extreme hunger."

The caravan increased or diminished as groups of families joined it or fell away. At one time, when musk oxen and caribou were plentiful, there were as many as 600 Indians. It is evident that they went as they pleased. And Hearne patiently, uncomplainingly followed, until in August, six months after leaving Churchill, his quadrant was knocked over and smashed. Without it he could not fix his latitude, so he turned back to get another instrument.

During his long return journey he was plundered by strange Indians and would have been in a very serious position if he had not met Matonabbee—"The famous Leader", as he calls him. He was in effect Hearne's leader from that moment on. He was an Indian of splendid physique, considerable intelligence, great strength of mind and a little sensitivity. He had for some time been in contact with Prince of Wales Fort, bringing the Indians down to trade. He had some words of English, spoke the native dialects, and had great influence among the natives.

Matonabbee saw Hearne safely back to Churchill, where the young Englishman had twelve days of comparative rest and then was off again with another (old and inferior) surveying instrument. Matonabbee planned the route and made plain the reason for the previous failures. To quote from Hearne's *Journey*, "He attributed all our misfortunes to the misconduct of our guides, and the very plan we persued, by the desire of the Governor, in not taking any women with us on this journey, was, he said, the principal thing that occasioned all our wants: for, said he, when all the men are heavy laden they can neither hunt nor travel any considerable distance; and in case they meet with success in hunting, who is to carry the produce of their labour? Women, added he, were made for labour; one of them can carry or haul as much as two men can do. They also pitch our tents, make and mend our clothing, and keep us warm at night . . . . Women, though they do everything, are maintained at a trifling expense; for as they always stand cook, the very licking of their fingers in scarce times is sufficient for their subsistence."

Matonabbee knew what he was talking about: he had seven wives.

Instead of leading Hearne north-westward, along the route he had previously taken, Matonabbee chose a route that avoided much of the Barren Lands and took advantage of the sheltering forest, where there was game. Only when the winter was over did he swing north, taking Hearne towards the Coppermine river.

In May 1771, the upper waters of the river were approached and the Indian party, by then swollen to about 200, set about building birch-bark canoes. They also made shields. Hearne, who had for so long been trying to reach and explore the river to its mouth, learned that his companions' intention was to attack the Eskimos near the coast.

A paragraph from his book sums up how purposefully he faced up to his role as a white man alone among a savage people on whom he was entirely dependent, and with a specific objective in mind. Let he who is without fear fire the first arrow.

"When I was acquainted with the intentions of my companions, and saw the warlike preparations that they were carrying on, I endeavoured as much as possible to persuade them from putting their inhuman design into execution; but

so far were my entreaties from having the wished-for effect it was concluded I was
actuated by cowardice; and they told me, with great marks of derision, that I was
afraid of the Esquimaux. As I knew my personal safety depended in a great
measure on the favourable opinion they entertained for me in this respect, I was
obliged to change my tone, and replied, that I did not care if they rendered the
name and race of the Esquimaux extinct; adding at the same time, that though I
was no enemy to the Esquimaux, and did not see the necessity of attacking them
without cause, yet if I should find it necessary to do it, for the protection of any one
of my company, my own safety out of the question, so far from being afraid of a
poor defenceless Esquimaux, whom I despised more than feared, nothing should
be wanting on my part to protect all who were with me. This declaration was
received with great satisfaction; and I never afterwards ventured to interfere with
any of their war-plans."

Leaving their women and children behind, the warriors went down river on
foot and by canoe to the Eskimo tents. It is clearly stated that Matonabbee, the
perfect Indian, was the leader of the tribally mixed band. Hearne went with them.

The Indians put on their war-paint and rushed the sleeping tents at one o'clock
in the morning when all the Eskimos were asleep. The massacre was complete
and there is no need to expand upon its horror. Hearne was deeply affected but
joined in the feast that followed.

"When we had finished our meal, which was the first we had enjoyed for many
hours, the Indians told me they were again ready to assist me in making an end of
my survey. It was then about five o'clock in the morning of the seventeenth [July],
the sea being in sight from the North West by West to the North East, about eight
miles distant. I therefore set instantly about commencing my survey, and persued
it to the mouth of the river, which I found all the way so full of shoals and falls that
it was not navigable even for a boat . . . . I am certain of it being the sea, or some
branch of it, by the quantity of whalebone and seal-skins which the Esquimaux
had at their tents . . . . The ice was not then broken up, but was melted away for
about three quarters of a mile from the main shore."

Thus was the north coast of the continent first reached by a white man. Hearne
set up a mark and claimed the area for the Hudson's Bay Company. The copper
mine proved to be of no commercial value, and no new trade resulted from the
journey. Hearne's achievement had a different significance: he had seen the
Canadian Arctic coast much further west than had any other white
man—beyond the longitude of Baffin Island and the north-western horn of
Hudson Bay. If this horn or the broken lands to the northward could be by-passed,
there was a possible way along the narrow strip of open water between the
continental coast and the July ice. Hearne was sadly disappointed that he had not
found the abundant copper and good trade prospects for which he had been
hoping, but in fact he had made an important geographical discovery—to be

Scenes from the author's own Arctic years: (TOP LEFT) the kayak was an easy way through the ice floes; (TOP RIGHT) washing in the Arctic was difficult except in summer; (BOTTOM LEFT) building an igloo, the cracks between the blocks were caulked with snow and a tunnel was dug for an entrance; (BOTTOM RIGHT) the author feeding the expedition dogs (*Scott Polar Research Institute*)

(RIGHT) The British were slow to use sledge dogs, they preferred using men, who were often expected to haul over 200 lb each. Here a frost-bite casualty is rescued (*Scott Polar Research Institute*). (BELOW) A game of cricket on ice. In the long Arctic night, every means was used to keep up morale. (BELOW RIGHT) Camping for the night: the tents were not effective for keeping out draughts. The man in the foreground is digging up snow for water while his fellows cook at an enormous, cumbersome stove (*Scott Polar Research Institute*).

S. Cabot

M. Frobisher

H. Hudson

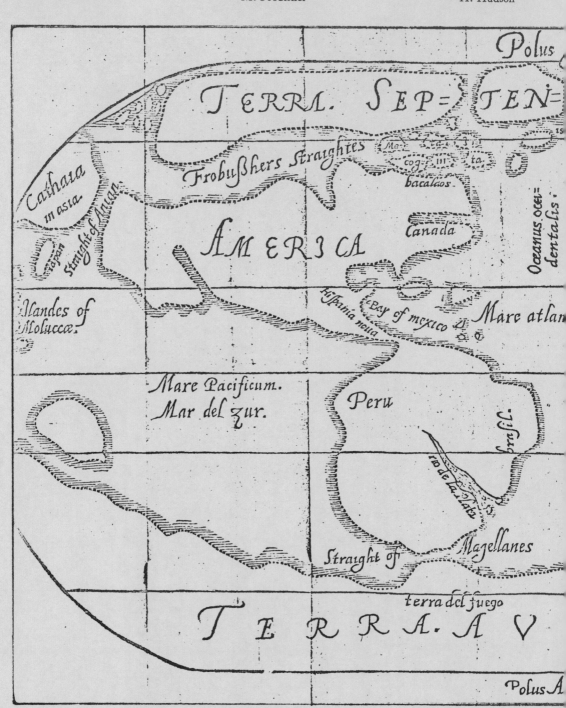

A map of 1578 following Frobisher's voyages and incorporating Frobisher's optimistic assessment of Arctic waterways

W. Parry

John Ross

J. Franklin

...us

...RIONA= LIS.

Circulus articus

tartaria *ob.fl.* *ASIA*

EVROPA *tanais fl.* *china*

mare caspum

e Mediterra... *Incum* *India*

tropicus Cancri

Arabia *MFRICA* *Red sea* *calecut* *Mare Eoum*

...unea *sinus*

Circulus aequinoctialis

montes Lunae *y. s. lawrentij* *Iaua maior*

tropicus capricorni

...nus *Australis*

...apo di buona speranza.

Circulus Antarticus

...TRALIS.

...s

Eskimo pillaging boats (*Mansell Collection*)

An Eskimo painting of Capt. John Ross's boats "Arctic Highlanders"

(ABOVE) An Eskimo woman; (OVERLEAF) Seal hunting by kayak

complemented seven years later by the findings of one of England's greatest explorers, who, by a mistake, sparked off a more useful exploration.

Captain James Cook was a world traveller. For a man who had looked for Antarctica (unsuccessfully) and explored Australia, New Zealand and the vast Pacific, a glance at the possibilities of the North-West Passage was a comparatively minor affair, not the great adventure of the pilots previously considered. On his third voyage (the season before he was murdered in Hawaii) Cook sailed through Bering Strait and had a look left and right. He did not go far in either direction, but to the eastward he reached what he with good reason called Icy Cape, a couple of hundred miles from the northern end of Bering Strait, and so identified a point at the western end of the North American Arctic coast. Hearne had reached the Arctic sea at a point about 1,200 miles away in a straight line to the eastward.

However, it was not how far Cook had gone, but what he had seen on the way, that sparked off interest. Cruising up the west coast of Alaska, he had passed an inlet that, because of the swift current, he supposed to be the estuary of a river. It was named Cook's river, and the explorer took possession of it in the name of the king.

By mistaking that wide inlet for the estuary of what might have been a large river, Cook lit a beacon for the men who were striving westward. What Groseilliers and Radisson had said had not been forgotten; and, even if there were no way for ships to the north-west, there might still be a freshwater route that would open up the Pacific coast to the fur trade. The traders were legion. Besides the Hudson's Bay Company there were the associations that merged into the North-West Company, and there were what the bigger concerns called the Pedlars, the individuals. These were not trappers. They tried to get ahead of each other in opening up new areas to trade with the Indians, and to this end established numerous trading posts and frequently quarrelled (often bloodily) among themselves. At first the thrusters were French Canadians and Englishmen. After Canada had become British they were principally Scots. The Scots got on better with the enduring French element, and perhaps with the Indians also. The life suited them.

In such country it is possible to go almost anywhere by canoe, provided one is skilled enough. However, where there are rapids too steep to ascend even by poling, or too violent to run, or when it becomes necessary to transfer from one waterway to another, portages are needed. This means dividing the canoe's contents into man-loads and laboriously transporting them—perhaps making several trips back and forth. Finally the canoe must be transported and everything reloaded. This makes canoe transport over long distances strenuous in the extreme, and there is always the problem of finding sufficient food.

The first explorer fully to exploit canoe transport was Alexander Mackenzie, a Scot from Stornaway in the Outer Hebrides. He arrived at his company's post on

Lake Athabasca, deep in the interior of Canada, in October 1787. During his first winter there he heard stories from the Indians about a wide river that flowed north-westward from the Great Slave Lake. The possible connection between this and "Cook's river" fired the young man's imagination, and he determined to find the river and trace its course.

He set off from Fort Chipewyan on Lake Athabasca on 3 June 1789. His party, which travelled in birch-bark canoes, consisted of four Canadians, two of whom were accompanied by their Indian wives, a German, and an Indian leader called English Chief, who had formerly been a member of Matonabbee's band and who had with him his two wives and two of his followers, who were to act as hunters. As a basic ration the party carried pemmican, dried venison. They never went hungry.

The way to the Great Slave Lake was devious but already known. Mackenzie reached it on 9 June. It was still largely frozen over, and it took him twenty days to find the effluent channel on the western side. Thereafter he ran the river in thirteen days. The possible dangers depended mainly on the reaction of the unknown Indian tribes—the Slave or Beavers, Dogribs, Quarrellers or Squint-eyes—who might have imagined they were being attacked. But Mackenzie handled them perfectly. They appeared never to have seen a white man before and possessed a minimum of metal. Their hooks were made of bone, their lines of reindeers sinew, their cooking vessels (heated by dropping hot stones into them) of tightly woven basket-work. Their weapons were bows and arrows.

Mackenzie's style is tense, sometimes telegraphic, but he gives a sufficient picture of the virgin country through which he so swiftly paddled. He praised his men. On 12 July, when stopped by ice, he noted, "My men express much sorrow that we are obliged to return without seeing the sea, in which I believe them sincere for we marched exceeding hard coming down the river and I never heard them grumble; but on the contrary in good spirits, and hope every day that the next would bring them to the *Mer d'Ouest* . . . ."

In fact they were already there—or rather on the northern coast. The frozen lake that Mackenzie supposed he had reached was the Arctic sea. This was confirmed when during the night the tide rose and flooded his baggage.

Alexander Mackenzie was knighted for his achievement, but he called the river that now bears his name the Disappointment. Like Hearne, a fellow trader, he did not appreciate the geographical importance of fixing a point on the unknown Arctic coastline.

He concluded his Journal, "It was in the summer of 1789 that I went this expedition in hopes of getting into Cook's River; tho' I was disappointed in this it proved without a doubt that there is not a North West Passage below this latitude and I believe it will generally be allowed that no passage is practicable in a higher latitude the Sea being eternally covered with Ice."

Three years after reaching the mouth of the Mackenzie, this determined man did manage to cross to the Pacific. Shortness of time and damage to his canoe by the furious rivers of the Rocky Mountains compelled him to finish the journey by a seventeen-day march; but he had proved to his own satisfaction that it could be done—although by a route that could not be described as a passage.

Chapter 16

The Motive Changes

The explorers discussed in the last chapter were still influenced by the hope that a commercially valuable northern route to the Pacific existed. Their experiences were the final proof that, as such, the North-West Passage did not exist. Yet in the reign of George III the government for the first time offered a reward for the discovery of the Passage—no less than £20,000. Why did it do so? The point of view was altering and the new motive became clear when the Napoleonic wars were at last over.

It was so different from earlier motives that the story takes on a new character. Paradoxically, it may seem, there was a far wider and more lively interest in the Passage: in just one generation far more money, ships and lives were committed to the cause than in all the previous centuries of exploration. The reason, to put it at its simplest, was the feeling that the age-old mystery, which had started in the heyday of wool, had *got* to be unravelled; that proud, all-powerful Britain must finish the task to which she had set her hand.

There was more to it in detail, of course. The press and public were intensely interested, the Royal Geographical Society and Royal Society scientifically so. The Navy was restless for adventure and achievement, supremely confident. In 1818 the Admiralty equipped four whalers of between 250 and 400 tons. The *Dorothea* and *Trent*, commanded by Captain David Buchan and Lieutenant John Franklin, were despatched by the North Pole route; and the *Isabella* and *Alexander*, commanded by Captain John Ross and Lieutenant Edward Parry, were sent via Davis Strait to find and penetrate the North-West Passage. All the officers and men, except perhaps the youngest midshipman, had more than proved themselves in war. The commanders' instructions included details of what they were to do when they met in the Pacific.

The *Dorothea* and *Trent* got no further north than had Hudson's little *Hopewell*. The heavy pack of the landless polar ocean was impenetrable by sailing ships of any size.

John Ross made a tour of Baffin Bay, handsomely restoring the reputation of the great navigator who had found and charted it two centuries before. Ross might have done much more, for he entered Lancaster Sound and sailed up it fifty miles. It was a most promising waterway, deep, steep-sided, thirty miles broad, and in that season unobstructed by ice. But then—as he later described in his book—he "distinctly saw the land round the bottom of the bay forming a chain of mountains connected with those which extended along the north and south sides". He sketched them, and named them Crocker Mountains. John William Crocker was flesh and blood, but almost from the first there was considerable doubt about the reality of the mountains called after him.

It is worth mentioning that the Arctic has throughout history been littered with bits of non-existent topography. The Zeno map, showing a dozen lands that are not there, is the classic example. That might have been conscious fiction, but Busse Island, on the other hand, was not. It was seen throughout a century by about as many people as failed to find it. An even more striking example is Crocker Land (only by coincidence named like the Crocker Mountains), seen by Peary from Ellesmere Island, far to the north, during his attempt to reach the Pole in 1906. A later expedition, led by Commander Donald MacMillan, went in search of it, proved it was not there, and then saw it in the distance from the cairn from which Peary had seen it. "Mirage" is the one-word explanation. The Arctic has its hallucinatory oases. In high latitudes refraction plays strange tricks. I have myself seen ghosts of mountains standing on their heads on top of existing peaks, and features that were below the horizon lifted above it. You cannot always believe your eyes. Captain Ross must be excused for seeing the Crocker Mountains.

The Admiralty and the Royal Geographical Society thought otherwise. There was as yet no proof that Captain Ross was wrong in believing Lancaster Sound to be blocked by mountains; but Sir John Barrow, the Secretary of the Admiralty, and Sir Joseph Banks, President of the Royal Geographical Society, were convinced that he had erred. Curiously, there does not appear to have been any firm evidence one way or the other from the officers of the *Isabella* (they were said all to have been at dinner!), while the *Alexander* was too far astern to see. The consequent controversy is interesting in that it was so wide and so heated. Not only were those in official positions concerned, but, in addition, the press and public became excited about it. The failure of Captain Buchan and Lieutenant Franklin to sail over the North Pole was accepted calmly. The Pole had not yet emerged as a point of achievement, only as a possible signpost to the Orient. But the North-West Passage stirred the blood and the imagination. Thousands of words were printed about the book that John Ross published in 1819 (the year after his return!), and few of them were as friendly as those that appeared in the *Edinburgh Review*, whose editor sprang to the defence of his compatriot. An extract from the *Edinburgh* article is given below, and incidentally shows the extent of geographical ignorance only a century and a half ago. One of the world's seven continents, Antarctica, had not yet been found and it was not known if the opposite polar area was covered by sea or broken lands. The pro-Passage creed was that there existed a way through the broken lands to a polar basin and thence to Bering Strait and the Pacific.

"For our parts, we have no objection to a Polar Basin—provided only that it can be found. But we cannot be brought to consider it as an article of prime necessity—and do not yet see why we should be out of humour either with Nature or our Navigators, although it should turn out that there was no such thing. It is curious indeed to see how fashions change—and how little more reasonable we are for all our learning. In the days of Captain Cook, all the world was for a Polar Continent—a Terra Australis; and yet we do not remember that any body abused that great navigator for failing to discover it, or reporting that it did not exist. Now, however, the rage is for a Polar Basin—and, we think, there are evident symptoms of very ungrateful dissatisfaction with Captain Ross and his associates, because they have exposed themselves to great toils and perils, with the same negative success. But in truth it is absurd to hold that there can be any want of success in an actual survey of regions previously unexplored—or that it can make any difference to the cause of geographical science, with what substances such regions may be bounded. It would have been a discovery if Captain Cook had found an Austral Continent, and it would have been a discovery if Captain Ross had found a North-West Passage. But if it was a discovery in the former to ascertain that there was no such land, it must be equally so in the latter to have ascertained that there is no such passage. The one found only ice where his employers hoped he might find land—and the other found only land, where they had set their hearts upon his finding water. But both have equally extended our actual knowledge of the globe, and enabled us to determine with precision much that was formerly disputed."

Sir John Barrow pressed for another expedition—to be led not by John Ross (he was never again given a ship by the Admiralty), but by his second-in-

command, Edward Parry. Two sturdy Royal Navy ships were provided, the *Hecla*
(375 tons) and the *Griper* (130 tons). Parry was under thirty years old, most of his
officers were still younger than he, and his midshipmen were in their teens. All
hands received double pay (for the first time on record for a North-West Passage
voyage) and were abundantly equipped with warm clothing, wolfskin blankets,
good food, and malt for beer-making. The ballast was coal. No expense was
spared. When the Lords of Admiralty set about something they did it handsomely,
and the public was behind the adventurers as it would have been in war.

Enthusiasm was the keynote of Parry's first expedition. The two ships sailed
through Lancaster Sound, through the mirage of Crocker Mountains, and, after a
probe southwards down what was named Prince Regent Inlet, continued
westward through the broken lands, officers and seamen crowding the rigging to
look eagerly ahead, discovering new islands evey day.

In Melville Sound they crossed the 110th meridian, so winning a bounty of
£5,000. By this time they were 30° west of the entrance to Lancaster Sound, and
only 15° east of the western limits of the maze of islands. However, though it
appears from a map that there is a clear waterway leading from Melville Sound
through to the Beaufort Sea (into which the Mackenzie river issues), the absence
of land does not mean absence of ice. With winter closing in, the two ships took
shelter on the south of Melville Island.

The wintering was entirely successful. The men were kept busy, well exercised
and well fed. A periodical was published, a school organized, and theatricals,
concerts and an operetta entitled "The North-West Passage" were performed.
The genial Parry, almost as accomplished with the fiddle as in navigation, set the
tune and maintained morale.

But when they tried to continue their westerly course the following season, it
became evident that the gods of the North-West Passage had been leading them
on by cunning tactics and lying in wait to crush their ships. Beyond Melville Sound
lay the Beaufort Sea—with its limitless weaponry of heavy ice floes, a moving
stream of huge fragments many years old and fathoms thick. Another part of the
vast concentration that had prevented the Pole from being approached through
Spitsbergen waters now made it impossible to press westward beyond the maze of
islands. More than that, the pack was advancing south-eastwards through the
wider channels of the maze.

Parry returned to England with the conviction that, if it were going to be
possible to reach Bering Strait, the gateway to the Pacific, by means of a sea
passage round the top of North America, it would be by following the continental
coastline as closely as possible and so seeking to obtain the maximum protection
that the broken lands could afford against the pack, for as far west as they
extended. However, between Icy Cape and Hudson's Bay, only two points on this
coastline had been reached: the Mackenzie delta and the mouth of the

Coppermine river. The coast might be explored by land, but any seaborne exploration had to rely on finding a passage.

The search for the Passage thus entered a new phase: a combination of landborne coastal exploration (considered in the next chapter) and attempts to find a sea route through to the vital stretch of coast. Perhaps the key was a channel leading southward from Lancaster Sound; or did Hudson Bay have the answer after all? Parry led what was to be the final exploratory voyage to Hudson Bay.

There was no difficulty at that time in launching expeditions. Not only was the Admiralty still keenly interested, but the general public too had become enthralled. The search, with its hopes and disappointments, its incidents of courage and danger and descriptions of an unknown scene, was like a serial story with long intervals between instalments. The Royal Navy was in charge; there were no more mutinies or strikes. So popular were the commanders (even loved) that, after first having taken the Arctic unseen (to use a schoolboy phrase), the same officers and seamen volunteered again and again and soon were at home in the new surroundings. They took much longer—a generation—to begin taking advantage of the Eskimos' experience (a thing the early explorers had not thought of) and to learn from them something of how to live and travel in comfort in the Arctic. Parry's men, among others, learned the hard way, as one example will show. While wintering on Melville Island, Parry took a party exploring to the northern shore, and with them they trundled along a hand-cart. This—inevitably—broke; so they used it as fuel to cook their supper and had to carry seventy-pound loads on their backs.

The ships that Parry commanded in his exploration of Hudson Bay in 1821–3 were the *Fury* and *Hecla*. With them he penetrated and thoroughly examined the sound between Southampton Island and the western mainland (not quite conclusively examined by Middleton). Then the coast to the northward was scientifically searched, the ships' boats poking into every inlet, until, at the north-western corner of Foxe Basin, they reached the only water passage other than Hudson Strait that leads out of these otherwise landlocked waters. It was a channel two miles wide, blocked as tightly with ice as a bottleneck with cork. The finest thing about this permanently choked canal is its name: Fury and Hecla Strait.

After two winters in the ice Parry arrived at the decision that this strait, had it been open, would have led to a waterway connection with Prince Regent Inlet and Lancaster Sound. In this he was right. His guess was backed by sketch maps that an intelligent Eskimo woman had drawn, showing Melville Peninsula (the western side of Foxe Basin) as a narrow strip of land with water beyond. Yet, correct as she was in this, her experience was local and she could not know that this water did not stretch to the mouth of the Coppermine river. Not knowing this, Parry decided to explore Prince Regent Inlet and, if possible, press south and west. At least, he thought, he should be able to link up with the land parties that were then exploring the continental coast.

He sailed again in the *Hecla* in 1824, with an old shipmate, Hopner, commanding the *Fury*, and James Ross (nephew of John) and others of his original midshipmen (now lieutenants) included in the company. Youth was still at the helm and enthusiasm was as high as ever. But it was a case of third time unlucky. The ice was against them all the way. They were battered in the Middle Pack and reached Lancaster Sound so late in the season that they had to winter at the northern end of Prince Regent Inlet, the first wide channel leading to the southward. They passed the dark months pleasantly enough, with excursions for exercise and masquerades for diversion; but the next season was one of continuous battle with an enemy that did not tire. No sooner were the ships released from the last winter's ice than they were attacked by masses of heavy pack, several years' freezing in thickness. The land in this area rises sheer from the sea. It was described as resembling "an immense wall in ruins". The crews of the *Fury* and *Hecla* fought for weeks, night and day, with their backs to this wall. Finally the *Fury*, broken beyond repair, was abandoned on the beach where she had grounded, and the exhausted men retreated in the *Hecla*.

Parry then left the north-west quadrant in order to make an attempt on the North Pole route in his trusty *Hecla*. His innovation was that, when the pack was reached, boats would be hauled over it (*boats*, not sledges). The loaded boats weighed 3,753 pounds each, which worked out at a haul of 268 pounds per man. Anyone who had dragged a dinghy over a muddy shore will conceive what the task was like on soft snow with forty-foot hummocks of ice to cross. After that voyage Parry became Hydrographer to the Admiralty.

The search among the ice floes was continued by others. Captain John Ross—rough, bluff and obstinate even in the face of Time—had for ten years been seeking an opportunity to redeem the mistake into which his eyes had tricked him in Lancaster Sound. Sir John Barrow and the Admiralty would have nothing more to do with him. But gin-maker Felix Booth—of the school of the merchant adventurers, though with no thought of material gain—gave him £18,000. With this the retired naval officer bought the 150-ton *Victory*, a sail-*cum*-paddle ferry boat that had been plying to the Isle of Man. He added the yeast of youth by taking as his second-in-command his nephew James Clark Ross, who had been with him in 1818 and who since then had been on all Parry's north-western voyages.

The *Victory* had taken a day on her trips between Liverpool and Douglas, and it is not to be supposed that her passengers had been particularly pleased with the accommodation she offered. In 1829 Captain Ross and his company took her to Baffin Bay, crossed the Middle Pack, sailed through Lancaster Sound and "Crocker Mountains", and then down Prince Regent Inlet. They spent three winters in her, and a fourth—having abandoned her—in such shelter as they could find. Her paddles drove her at three knots at best, and even so "the boilers also continued to leak, though we put dung and potatoes in them". This is an interesting augury, for it was only by automatic power that the Passage was finally pierced; and this first steamship in the North soon had her engine removed to save the space it occupied.

Ross sailed down Prince Regent Inlet in the hope of finding a waterway to lead him through to the unfettered continental coast, which was already being explored by land parties. But he failed to notice the narrow Bellot Strait—not surprisingly, for it was blocked by ice—and came to anchor in Lord Mayor's Bay amidst a large cluster of islands, which he drily named the Sons of the Clergy of the Church of Scotland. During the winter he occupied his men's minds by teaching the illiterate to read and write and the better-educated to navigate, and by lecturing both classes on total abstinence—which was a virtue forced upon them.

The Gulf of Boothia—the continuation of Prince Regent Inlet—proved to be a cul-de-sac. So, the *Victory* remaining ice-bound, only overland exploration remained feasible. During the following two seasons James Ross, with the help of Eskimos, made two important sledge journeys. He crossed to the western side of the peninsula, and then, without realizing it (owing to bad visibility), crossed a strait to King William Island, which he took to be an extension of the mainland and named King William Land. On reaching its north-western shore (along Victoria Strait) he noted the heaviest pack ice he had ever seen, and named two headlands Franklin and Jane Franklin. The north-eastern shore was shielded from this ice current, but shortage of food prevented him following it far, and bad visibility caused him to believe that it (Rae Strait) was a bay—in other words that King William Island was part of the mainland. As such he dotted it in upon his chart.

On his second long journey James Ross reached the Magnetic Pole, further to the northwards—the place where the compass stands on its head. This, when reported, was rightly hailed as a great scientific achievement; but the mistake that Ross had made about the coastline (which he had represented on his chart by a dotted line, but was later drawn solid by a cartographer) was seventeen years later to cost more than a hundred lives.

By the third winter it had become evident that the *Victory* was doomed; so during the dark days the carpenters built sledges. On these the ship's boats were dragged northwards in the spring.

The men reached Fury Beach, where the *Fury* had been wrecked on Parry's third expedition. The ship had disappeared, but a considerable stock of her canned stores remained. The men built a hut roofed with canvas, and Captain Ross named it Somerset House.

As soon as there was open water they set out by boat for Lancaster Sound. By October it was evident that they could not reach it. They dumped the boats, built sledges and retreated to Somerset House for a Christmas dinner of fox and water.

As soon as the ice began to break up again they returned to the boats and once more set sail. It was August (1833) before they had turned out of Prince Rupert Inlet and eastwards into Lancaster Sound, but, once there, they hoped to sight a whaler. On the 26th they saw one without her seeing them; but later the same day they saw another ship, were able to approach her, and at last were sighted. The ship sent off a boat commanded by the mate.

When the boats came within hail there was a conversation that was not only dramatic but also cast an interesting light on past events. The soundness of Captain Ross's eyesight had been questioned at the time of the Crocker Mountains controversy. Now he called out to the approaching boat to ask what ship she came from.

"The *Isabella* of Hull, once commanded by Captain Ross," answered the mate.

On reaching Britain, the Rosses and their crew were given an amazed and delighted welcome. Only two men had died, one from tuberculosis contracted before the expedition. The country knighted John Ross, returned Felix Booth his £18,000, and created him a baronet.

The public applauded and waited for the next instalment.

Chapter 17

Coastal Exploration

When the Navy started its assault on the Passage, the northern shore of Canada was unmapped. The continental coastline between Icy Cape, Alaska, and Hudson Bay—a stretch of well over 2,000 miles, as the crow flies—was blank except for two dots, at the mouths of the Mackenzie and Coppermine rivers.

For Britain it was a most unsatisfactory, even shameful, state of affairs. Ice thwarted survey of the islands, but there was no reason why the coast should not be explored. Canada was a great and developing colony. There was little sense in spending huge sums on offshore exploration before the mainland coast was known.

When Lieutenant John Franklin returned in the *Trent* from the ice-choked seas about Spitsbergen, he was lent to the Colonial Office to make a survey of the American Arctic coast. With him were seconded Dr Richardson, RN, in charge of natural-history work; two midshipmen, George Back and Robert Hood, who were both artists; and an able seaman named John Hepburn. The Admiralty was naturally most interested that this survey should be made, but that the Navy should provide the personnel was about as logical as it would have been to put an Army officer in command of a ship. For his first expedition, Franklin was given the task of travelling by land and river to the mouth of the Coppermine, and then exploring the coast by birch-bark canoe. It was hardly a naval command!

He and his companions from the British Isles (Richardson and Hepburn were Scottish) had no experience of Canadian travel; nor, with their background of naval discipline, had they the elasticity to handle independently-mined pioneers: the civilian employees of the Hudson's Bay Company and its rival the North-West Company. That they rose above these handicaps to do what they did is in itself a great achievement. If Franklin were not so well known for his last expedition, by sea, perhaps his tremendous land journeys would be better remembered than they are.

He led his men 1,500 miles to build what he named Fort Enterprise, his advanced base near the source of the Coppermine river. He had recruited a number of French Canadian voyageurs, including Michel, who spoke the Iroquois language; some Indian hunters and their wives (to do the sewing); and, as allies, the Coppermine tribe of Chief Akaitcho, who undertook to hunt in the neighourhood of Fort Enterprise and to stock it with game against the expedition's return. It was a mixed company with tenuous loyalties.

In June 1821, Franklin's party ran the Coppermine in birch-bark canoes. Within sight of the sea, at a place that they called Bloody Falls, they found a number of broken-boned skeletons, a grim confirmation of Hearne's story of the Eskimos massacred there. At this point Franklin sent the Indian hunters back under charge of a North-West Company clerk named Wentzel, with instructions to lay down caches of game on the way; he, meanwhile, with his countrymen and the voyageurs, would carry on to the sea.

The voyageurs were greatly disturbed by the sea, which they had never seen before. The coast was bare, with many islands. Across what was later named Coronation Gulf lay Victoria Island, larger than England and stretching north-ward to Melville Sound, which Parry had reached before being turned back by the big battalions of the polar pack.

Franklin had taken two years to reach his starting point, and now he had reached it he was faced with the question of how far eastward he could explore the coast before having to turn back. He had hoped to work along the coast as far as Hudson Bay, thereby determining conclusively the bay's relation with the coastline to the west. That he could not hope to achieve now, for the party's food stocks would allow, at most, only a few weeks' exploration. So the question: how far dare he go? He had been trained in a hard school: he had been under close fire at the battle of Copenhagen when he was only fourteen years old; he had been at Trafalgar and later had been wrecked off the north coast of Australia while surveying with Captain Flinders. Richardson was completely staunch and reliable. Young Back seemed to delight in arduous adventure, and was, in addition, a good mixer with a sense of humour, which permeates his writings. Of Hood we know less: he wrote nothing, only painted. One pictures him as poetic, idealistic. He certainly was not lacking in courage. John Hepburn was like Philip Staffe, the type of the faithful carpenter.

The voyageurs, on the other hand, were near to mutiny. Since they feared death, their good wages meant nothing to them.

Franklin reached as far east as what he called Point Turnagain, still under the shadow of Victoria Island. He had mapped 550 miles of coastline (including the many indentations), but, though a considerable distance, this represented only a small fraction of the Arctic shore. There remained a big blank east of Turnagain.

Being in a hurry, owing to shortage of food, Franklin aimed directly for Fort Enterprise, across the Barren Lands. He may have been right in thinking that to retrace his two-sided route would have been even more disastrous. There were twenty-one men in the party and they had a calculated 150 miles to walk. It was September, winter coming on fast, the country virtually without game and cruelly difficult to travel.

When things go wrong under such conditions, catastrophe is close. There were acts of heroism and self-sacrifice, as when Richardson tried to swim across a near-frozen river with a line and was finally pulled back numbed almost to death; and when Franklin fainted and was revived by the insistence of his companions that he should have the last of the precious preserved food. But there suddenly comes a level from which there is no resurrection. Several men lay down and died. Michel, who had previously earned a good character, took to cannibalism, and killed two or three men, including Hood, before Richardson shot him.

Back pushed on to Fort Enterprise, which the Indians had undertaken to stock with game. He found it empty and without stores. He left a note saying that he was going on southward to try to reach Fort Providence, which he estimated would take him fourteen days. He walked on, living on a pair of leather trousers, a gun cover, a shoe, the lichen called *tripe de roche*, and on the remains of a deer, to which he was guided by a "convocation" of wolves and crows. He came upon some Indians and sent back food. The net result was that, of the twenty-one who had set out upon the journey, eleven died. The expedition was expensive in life.

It had been a terrible story of muddle and unkept promises. A basic difficulty was eliminated by the amalgamation of the Hudson's Bay Company and the North-West Company. Travel and supply arrangements were likely to be easier in the future. But it is improbable that this influenced the decision of Franklin, Richardson, Back and Hepburn, soon after their return to England, to volunteer for further exploration in the north-west. There could scarcely be a better example of the compulsive nature of the search.

Franklin's second expedition, made in 1825–7, showed how everything, or nearly everything, can go right, given good organization and some luck. This time his plan was to descend the Mackenzie river and from its mouth to explore the coastline east and west. Meanwhile the *Blossom*, commanded by Captain Beechey, was to sail through Bering Strait from the Pacific and, by exploring beyond Cook's Icy Cape, attempt contact with Franklin's party. If the scheme had been fully successful, the coastline would thus have been surveyed from Bering Strait to the Coppermine, and beyond it to Turnagain.

Franklin again took with him Richardson and Back; a midshipman named Kendall replaced the murdered Hood; and for boat crews Franklin chose volunteer British seamen. The Hudson's Bay Company co-operated fully, lending one of their officers, Peter Dease, and supplying hunters. Fort Franklin was built on Great Bear Lake, about halfway between the Mackenzie and the Coppermine. Some preliminary surveying was achieved before the freeze-up. The winter months were passed in harmony and health.

Since the Mackenzie is a deeper and more disciplined river than the Coppermine, larger and stouter craft could be used. At the end of June, these carried the men to the apex of the delta in a matter of days. There Franklin and Back turned westwards in the *Lion* and *Reliance*, and Richardson and Kendall eastwards in the *Dolphin* and *Union*.

Richardson's party reached the Coppermine in five weeks, charting 900 miles of coastline on the way. At the mouth of the river they dumped their boats (a wonderful find for some wandering Eskimo!); then, turning inland, they walked to Great Bear Lake, reaching Fort Franklin before the other party.

While still in the delta Franklin had experienced an incident that was no less dangerous for containing an element of farce. Seeing a large Eskimo encampment on an island, he approached it to obtain local knowledge. A mile offshore the boats ran aground—and some 300 Eskimos came swarming out to them in kayaks. When the native interpreter in the *Lion* assured them that the white men were friendly, they closed in on the boats, mischievously snatching at everything on board. With difficulty and some risk, the boats escaped and the survey was begun.

The Alaskan coast proved shallow and exposed, and the weather was bad. Franklin got only about half way to Icy Cape, and Captain Beechey fell some 160 miles short of meeting him. This gap was more annoying than serious, for the trend and character of the coast showed that the way was open.

The gap at the eastern end, between Point Turnagain and Fury and Hecla Strait (Parry had by this time explored to the north-west corner of Foxe Basin), was several times greater and certainly more important, for this stretch of coast contained numerous indentations and peninsulas and impinged on the maze of islands. On his return to England the insatiable Franklin put forward two plans: to sledge westwards from the top of Hudson Bay to Point Turnagain; and to descend the unmapped Great Fish river (now called Back river), which rose in the neighbourhood of Great Slave Lake and presumably reached the coast somewhere to the east of Point Turnagain. Had this latter plan been approved, and proved successful, Franklin would have learned something to his later advantage, if not salvation. But for the moment the Admiralty had had enough of north-western exploration. Franklin was knighted and appointed governor of Tasmania (a post he held for seven years). He had remarried, his first wife having died, and with Lady Jane he might have comfortably completed an honourable career. That was not to be; but, before Franklin returned to the Arctic, others went there and added to knowledge of the coast. In the process, however, James Clark Ross made his fatal mistake about King William Island.

In the year when Franklin was knighted, 1829, Captain John Ross and his nephew sailed in the *Victory*. When they had been gone for two winters there was concern about them. After three there was acute anxiety. A private committee headed by George Ross, brother of John Ross, subscribed funds for a rescue attempt. Back was put in charge, with Dr Richard King as his critical and opinionated second-in-command. It is interesting that the intention was to approach the Arctic sea by way of Great Fish river, one of Franklin's plans. It was believed that Ross had intended to turn southward by Prince Regent Inlet, and it was possible that the unknown river might take Back's party to the southern extremity of this waterway, or near it.

During Franklin's first expedition, Back had shown himself the perfect second-in-command. He had saved the party from annihilation by pressing on by sheer will-power, his own life "a thing indifferent", but his sense of responsibility compelling him to press on until he found help. In action he never spared himself. He was of strong religious convictions and likeable temperament. For a student of the search he is a welcome change from so many of the other explorers, for he possessed a sense of humour and a gift for the vivid phrase. Above all, with his artist's eye he could appreciate the most savage aspects of nature.

The Great Fish river rushes, dodges and cascades through some 550 miles of barren, rocky land. Sometimes it draws breath in a lake—and the navigator is uncertain where to steer. Then it is off again on another wild adventure. But in Back's description it is also beautiful: "High rocks beetling over the rapids like towers, or rent into the most diversified forms, gay with various coloured mosses, or shaded by overhanging trees—now a tranquil pool, lying like a sheet of silver—now the dash and foam of a cataract."

Back had learned by courier shortly before starting on the descent that the Rosses were safely returned to England. The original purpose of his expedition therefore no longer applied; but, having come so far and wintered on Great Slave Lake, it would have been waste of energy and money not to explore to the sea—as Back did.

It is necessary to picture what Back saw from the wide estuary of the river—or would have in good visibility. To the north-west, beyond what is now called

Simpson Strait, lay James Ross's King William Land, the northern part of which
he had explored. To the north-east of the estuary stretched open water,
suggesting a channel in that direction. But Back, with the information that the
Victory expedition was safe, had received a copy of James Ross's chart, which
showed this open water blocked by an isthmus connecting King William Land
with the base of the Boothia Peninsula. Had Back not known that the Ross party
was safe, he would certainly have pressed north-east; and he would have made the
vital discovery that King William Land is an island. Dr King urged him to go
north-east; but Back's contingency orders were to turn west towards the
Coppermine, which he did. Unfortunately, he was unable to progress very far, and
so there remained gaps in what was known of the coast on either side of the
mouth of the Great Fish river.

The Hudson's Bay Company, which had fully co-operated with Back, undertook
to fill the blanks—including the gap in knowledge of the Alaskan coast, between
Franklin's farthest west and Captain Beechey's farthest east. The men chosen
were Peter Dease, who had built and looked after Fort Franklin on Great Bear
Lake during Franklin's second expedition, and Thomas Simpson, a much younger
man, with whom both Back and Franklin had failed to see eye to eye on the first
expedition.

Very few people got on well with Thomas Simpson, the notable exception
being his brother, Alexander, to whom he wrote long letters, generally in critical
terms about those with whom he had to deal. Born at Dingwall in Ross-shire, he
had graduated at Aberdeen University and then emigrated to Canada, where he
quickly made a name as an intelligent and amazingly energetic fur trader. When
he was chosen as the strong right arm of Dease in 1836, he was twenty-eight years
old.

The first thing he did was to walk on snowshoes to what is now Winnipeg to
take a course in surveying. He made the round trip of 1,300 miles alone, covering
up to fifty miles a day, and returned to join Dease on the day he had said he would.

Dease and Simpson left a party to build a base on Great Bear Lake while they
descended the Mackenzie and turned westward along the coast. Any second
expedition has the advantage of the experience of the first, and they travelled
more quickly than had Franklin. But beyond his farthest west they encountered
the combined obstacles of shallow water, fog and ice. Simpson completed the
journey on foot, and on 4 August, "with indescribable emotions", sighted Point
Barrow, which Captain Beechey had reached from the opposite direction. "Mine
alone is the victory", wrote Simpson, the second-in-command.

He had caught the exploring fever, which does not always bring out a man's
best qualities. He was jealous of his predecessors and determined to out-do them.
He disparaged the pioneering that had made his own journey easier. He called
Dease "a worthy, indolent, illiterate soul".

After returning to Great Bear Lake, he spent the winter in furious activity, simply unable to rest. Walking in snowshoes, he covered a thousand miles or so, looking for the local Indians and searching over the Dismal Lakes for the best way to take the boats to the navigable waters of the Coppermine.

In 1838 he and Dease went down the Coppermine (one begins to name Simpson first, for the commander was already begining to consider himself a supernumerary). From the river mouth they got no further east than Point Turnagain, though Simpson made a dash of another hundred miles on foot.

Dease had by now had enough; but Simpson insisted on another year of exploration. So they cached the boats on the Coppermine, returned to base for the winter, and then tried again. On this occasion Simpson sailed past Point Turnagain and through Simpson Strait, the channel three miles wide that runs between King William Island and the mainland coast. He explored much of the southern shore of the island, but, like Back, did not get far enough to make the vital discovery that there was no land linking the island to Boothia.

He might have done so on an expedition that he projected—to follow the coast on to Fury and Hecla Strait; but he did not at once obtain approval for his plans. This apparent snub by his direct superior in Canada finally unbalanced the mind of this overworked and over self-confident man. He set off to appeal personally to the London headquarters—which meant travelling the first thousand miles on foot. He was accompanied by four half-breeds. He suddenly took it into his head that two of these intended to murder him, and shot them dead. He himself was later found in his tent with the back of his head blown off. It was as thought the gods of the North-West Passage, seeing their secrets endangered by an impudent human, had first driven him mad and then destroyed him.

George Back, although not destroyed, was broken by his exertions before he was forty—"burnt out" was his own expression. But he made one more expedition. In 1836 Captain Back (as he by then was) returned to a sailor's natural element to pilot the *Terror* into Hudson Bay. This was in pursuance of the second of Franklin's unaccepted plans: to land a boat-*cum*-sledge party at the head of one of the inlets behind Southampton Island, and thence proceed overland to trace the coastline west.

It was a bold plan and might have succeeded, had it not been that the gods of the North-West Passage were taking no chances. The *Terror* was gripped, undermined and squeezed by ice, which shivered her timbers in the most frightful manner. When at last she was released in the following season, all she could possibly hope for was to get home before the invading water broke down the strength of the crew who manned the pumps.

Early one morning, with the coast of Ireland dimly in sight, the First Officer knocked on the door of the Back's cabin, and, according to Sir Clements Markham, the following dialogue took place.

"Captain Back, Sir!"

"Yes, what is it?"

"The ship's sinking."

"Very good, Smyth, call me again at eight bells."

The *Terror* was run aground in Lough Swilly. This was Back's last voyage, but the *Terror* was repaired and lived to sail under the command of James Clark Ross to the Antarctic before dying in an all-out assault on the North-West Passage—*before* the coastal survey had been completed.

Chapter 18

The Most Impelling Motive

The *Erebus* and *Terror*, under the command of Sir John Franklin and with a total company of 129 officers and men—most carefully selected from a host of eager volunteers—sailed from the Thames on 19 May 1845, provisioned for three years. They anchored briefly off Disco Island in west Greenland. In late July they communicated with a whaler in Baffin Bay and parted from her on a course for Lancaster Sound.

As it was unlikely that any news would be heard of the expedition before a year was out, the fact nothing was heard during 1846 caused no undue anxiety; but in the open season of 1847 word was urgently awaited. As none had arrived by September, rescue plans were set in hand, and in 1848 the search began. Thereafter, it was maintained at high pressure for six years, in the belief that two stout vessels and 129 men could not have vanished without trace where there were so many islands and narrow channels. But they had. In March 1854 the Admiralty, by then preoccupied by the naval problems of the Crimean War, wrote off the *Erebus* and *Terror* and removed the men's names from the Navy List. The official opinion was that everything possible—or justifiable—had been done. A score of vessels had searched the channels of the maze, sledge parties had examined the islands where shipwrecked men might have camped or left records, and what was considered the likeliest part of the continental coast had been travelled. Now the public were reading the long casualty lists from Sebastopol; but the mystery of the North-West Passage was still at the back of their minds.

For the Franklin search had, inevitably, also been a continuation of the search for the Passage—since that was what he had been looking for. This has been compared with a serial story, from the British public's point of view, and it had been made all the more compelling by the added mystery. For us it is still a magnificent record of arctic exploration, with a dramatic ending. But, largely because the geography of the scene is so complex, unfolding all the time over so long a period, it is difficult for a modern reader to follow. It is much simplified if, so to speak, we look at the last page first. Thereby we lose the stimulus of mystery felt by the contemporary British and North American world. But we gain by being able to see how far away, and in a few cases how near, the searchers were to the primary object of their quest. There is a risk of judging unfairly with the aid of hindsight, but that is preferable to the danger of getting lost oneself.

Even so it will be as well to stylize the muddle of islands into something familiar as a town plan. There is a thoroughfare from Baffin Bay westward to the Beaufort Sea, which is part of the Polar Basin and stretches without further land to Bering Strait and Asia. This thoroughfare changes its name three times—from Lancaster Sound to Barrow Strait, then to Melville Sound and finally to McClure Strait. Lancaster Sound runs between Devon Island (to the north) and Baffin Island. The first turn to the left (south) is Prince Regent Channel, between Baffin Island and Somerset Island. It leads into the cul-de-sac Gulf of Boothia. But the channel has an alleyway to either side—ice permitting. Fury and Hecla Strait connects it with Hudson Bay, and Bellot Strait with the next turn to the left. This second turn between Somerset Island and Prince of Wales Island is Peel Sound, narrow but important. Important because it becomes Franklin Strait which converges on McClintock Channel, the third turn to the left.

The only turn to the right (north) which needs to be mentioned by name is Wellington Channel, almost opposite Peel Sound. Here the thoroughfare is called Barrow Strait. Beyond, westward, it rapidly widens into the great piazza of Melville Sound, which is bounded by Prince of Wales Island and Victoria Island on the southern side and Melville Island to the north. McClure Strait, between Banks (the most westerly island) and Melville Island, is the termination of the thoroughfare.

But from the point of view of ice traffic it is the beginning, or the main entrance. For the pack comes from the overcrowded Polar Ocean and Beaufort Sea and with the wind and current tends to travel east or south-eastwards. Advancing through McClure Strait and other channels on the northern side it concentrates in Melville Sound. But the possible exits are comparatively narrow. Sometimes

Barrow Strait and Lancaster Sound are completely blocked by the irresistible eastward drift. But most of the heavy pack goes down McClintock Channel and tries to squeeze its way through Victoria Channel between King William Island and the southeast corner of Victoria Island. The result is a chaotic ice jam, made still worse by shoals on which the biggest floes are stranded. The heavy pack does not manage to reach the coastal waters, which therefore become navigable as soon as the local ice of the previous winter has melted.

Franklin had told his wife, Lady Jane, that the best chance of making the Passage would be by hugging the continental coast. He had to get there, of course, beyond the reach of the heavy pack; but, before he began his final expedition, sufficient information had come to light for him to be able to choose a course.

Obeying his official instructions he sailed up Lancaster Sound and into Barrow Strait. Then he turned north up Wellington Channel and spent the rest of the summer exploring to the northward. One must suppose that Barrow Strait was full of ice and Wellington Channel clear. He wintered on Beechey Island, at the mouth of the channel. Three men died during the winter. A cairn was built on the highest point of the island, but apparently no written record was cached—none was ever found.

When the *Erebus* and *Terror* sailed from winter quarters in 1846 they did so in a hurry (equipment scattered on Beechy Island suggest this). Very likely the ice in their winter harbour was driven out by a sudden storm, the ships with it, and the crews had to jump aboard like men catching a moving train. The disposition of the pack (always unpredictable) must have dictated the vessels' course, and it was this that threw the searchers off the scent. Franklin went southward down Peel Sound, the narrowest turn to the south, which happened in that particular season to be navigable.

On reaching the junction of Franklin Strait (the continuation of Peel Sound) and McClintock Channel, Franklin might have made an east-about detour round King William Island to the continental shore, thus avoiding the ice jam in Victoria Strait. That was the way Amundsen went when he succeeded in navigating the Passage half a century later. But Franklin's charts showed King William Land, as it was then called, connected to the base of the Boothia Peninsula—no one had righted the error that James Clark Ross had made and the cartographers compounded. So Franklin turned into Victoria Strait. There his ships were caught, squeezed and held by the all-powerful pack a dozen miles from shore.

It was there that he and his men passed their second winter. They were being drifted very slowly on their way, which must have given them false hope; but the ice masses that held them were themselves being crushed by their own enormous weight and would never let them go.

Within sight of what, eighteen years previously, James Clark Ross had named

Cape Franklin, Sir John Franklin died on 11 June 1847. His men spent a third winter (1847–8) in the ships, and then tried to save themselves on foot.

Unfortunately, the ice had laid hold on the ships in the most awkward place, and the men were as distant as they could be from any outpost. They were too far south to make for Lancaster Sound, as John Ross had done; the Hudson's Bay Company posts in the Mackenzie delta were too far to the west—although, in fact, Dr John Rae of the Hudson's Bay Company was engaged in a geographical survey just a hundred miles or so away. To the southward the route to civilization lay round King William Island, across Simpson Strait to the continental shore, and up the Great Fish river. Nobody could suppose—or only one man did—that Franklin would choose to cross the Barren Lands again; and no one in England knew that Franklin was dead.

In June 1848, a year after Franklin's death, the *Enterprise* and *Investigator* sailed for Lancaster Sound with Sir James Clark Ross in command. It proved impossible to sail further than the end of the sound, for Barrow Strait and Prince Regent Inlet were blocked; but in the spring of 1849 a sledge party from the ships reached the depot at Fury Beach, which Franklin's men would certainly have visited if they had made for Lancaster Sound on foot. A second sledge party, led by Ross and including Lieutenant Leopold McClintock, a novice to the north, found and descended Peel Sound as far as their strength and stores allowed, but not far enough for them to learn that this jumble of pack ice was in fact the right trail. In the autumn, having found no trace of Franklin, the two ships were driven back down Lancaster Sound by the pack, and so returned to England.

Ross's expedition had been one of three sent out by the Admiralty to search the Arctic for Franklin. Of the others, one was charged to tackle the problem from Bering Strait, and one, led by Dr John Richardson, was given orders to proceed down the Mackenzie and explore eastwards from its delta. Neither produced any answers. Richardson covered most of the coast between the Mackenzie and the Coppermine, but it was the estuary of the Great Fish river, much further east, that held the key to the mystery. Dr Richard King, who had been Back's troublesome and critical second when he had descended that river a dozen years before, stated that this was the route by which Franklin would try to escape. Throughout 1847 he bombarded the Colonial Office and the Arctic Council of the Admiralty with demands that he should be enabled to lead a party down the Fish. He was vociferous in the press. He was right but he was rude. He was ignored.

In 1850 there was an explosion of activity. The Admiralty offered a reward of £20,000 to anyone finding the lost ships and men, and thirteen vessels were sent to search for them. Nine of these were commissioned by the Admiralty. The rest (an expression of the wide interest in and concern at Franklin's fate) joined the hunt under private sponsorship. James Ross had retired from the polar field after his voyage of 1848–9, but his uncle John, aged seventy-two, left his beloved North

West Castle on Loch Ryan in order to captain the schooner *Felix*, which was provided by Felix Booth and other individuals. Henry Grinnell, an American businessman, equipped the *Advance* and *Rescue* under Lieutenant De Haven, his officers and men renouncing before they sailed any claim to the reward. And Lady Jane Franklin fitted out the *Prince Albert*.

The general plan in 1850 was similar to that of two years previously, but on a much larger scale. Two flotillas were to advance towards each other from the extremities of the Passage. Thus, like the extended fingers of two hands, they would grope until they met among the straits and channels of the maze. The ships, of course, could advance only while there was open water, but during the long frozen period the new technique of sledging would be employed.

The *Plover* was permanently stationed off the Alaskan coast, with the *Herald* supplying her and cruising nearby. Captain Richard Collinson in the *Enterprise* and Commander Robert McClure in the *Investigator* were sent by way of the Horn to Bering Strait in order to make the advance from the western end. Since their approach route was so extended, the account of their achievements belongs later in our story, as does the account of Dr John Rae's renewed explorations in the uncharted gap of the continental coast.

Captain Horatio Austin commanded the flotilla of nine Royal Navy ships that tackled the problem from the east. Entering the Passage at Lancaster Sound, the flotilla sailed through to Barrow Strait, and at Beechey Island, at the mouth of Wellington Channel, found Franklin's first winter quarters. A cairn, scattered equipment and three graves marked the spot, but there was no message, no clue to Franklin's intentions. From there, assuming he had not turned back to the east, he could have sailed northwards, up Wellington Channel, or carried on westwards—perhaps continuing to Melville Sound or branching off southwards, down Peel Sound.

In the spring of 1851, 200 men fanned out in sledge parties, which travelled in eight different directions and covered some 7,000 miles in all. McClintock was organizer and leader of this mammoth achievement in man-hauling; and—noted Sir Clements Markham, who took part—"there were only three amputations of toes and one death from frostbite". But the only information about Franklin was negative. He had not visited Parry's winter harbour on Melville Island, which he would probably have done had he sailed west; and Peel Sound was judged unnavigable. Wellington Channel, however, was explored by ship and in the process a piece of charred wood was found.

Only Lady Franklin's ship, the *Prince Albert*, went south from Lancaster Sound—into Prince Regent Inlet. William Kennedy of the merchant navy was in command. His second was Lieutenant Réné Bellot, a French volunteer, and among the crew was John Hepburn, the faithful seaman of Franklin's coastal survey. He had followed his leader to Tasmania and then come back to join in the search for him. On a winter sledge journey Bellot found the strait named after him—the mile-wide channel between Somerset Island and Boothia—and in the summer the *Prince Albert* sailed through it. Kennedy's instructions were to press southward, and Bellot urged him to. Had he done so he would have passed through Franklin Strait and would almost certainly have sighted the *Erebus* and *Terror*, deserted but containing vital records. Instead he turned northwards, up Peel Sound, and so missed the ships by a matter of a hundred miles.

There was a still nearer miss when Dr Rae, working from the continental coast, went up Victoria Strait. He must have come very close to the line that Franklin's retreating crews had taken.

The fact was, however, that near-misses did not count; and, had it not been that no news had been heard of the *Enterprise* and the *Investigator*, which Collinson and McClure had taken through Bering Strait to search from the west, the Admiralty would now have closed the Franklin files. Instead, in 1852, it sent out five more ships, and gave the commander of the flotilla, Sir Edward Belcher, instructions to look for Collinson and McClure as well as for Franklin. Curiously, however, their Lordships (who have been unkindly criticized for their behaviour at this period) instructed Belcher that there should be no exploration to the southward of Barrow Strait and that "all the energy of the expedition be directed towards the upper portion of Wellington Strait"—where the piece of charred wood had been found.

Nothing whatever was discovered about the *Erebus* and *Terror* (although amazing sledge journeys were made—including one, by McClintock, of over 1,400 miles), but by a happy chance McClure's *Investigator* was found at an extremely critical moment.

The *Enterprise* and *Investigator*, when they sailed from England in January 1850, had been instructed to keep together in the ice. But McClure, a man of great drive and determination, raced Collinson (his superior) to Bering Strait. When Kellet (also his superior) signalled from the watchdog *Herald*, "Had you not better wait forty-eight hours?", he replied, "Important duty. Cannot on my own responsibility"—and plunged into the search.

Probing perilously between ice and shore, the *Investigator* rounded Point Barrow and followed the coast eastwards to beyond the Mackenzie delta, her interpreter frequently questioning Eskimo communities but receiving no information about Franklin.

When the ice at last eased, McClure set a course north-westward, reached Banks Island, and began working his way up the narrow channel (later to be called Prince of Wales Strait) that divides it from the northern end of Victoria Island. The force of the drifting ice encountered was tremendous, tossing the ship about like a plaything; but McClure forced his way along until he was within sixty miles of where the strait links up with Melville Sound. At that point he was only about a hundred miles from Parry's furthest west, on Melville Island; but new ice, cementing the floes together, prevented him from getting any further.

He wintered where he was, in a perilous situation, and tried again the following season. Still unable to advance, he turned about and made almost the complete circuit of Banks Island clockwise (so entering the strait that is now named after him) before reaching his second winter quarters: the Bay of Mercy, as he called it, on the north coast of Banks. In his journal he thanked God humbly for the possibility, almost the certainty, that it was he who had been chosen to realize—from the west—the age-old dream of sailing the North-West Passage.

But the heavy ice stream coming from the polar basin still lay between him and Melville Island, and only under the lee of that shore could he hope to sail eastwards to Lancaster Sound and thus complete the Passage by ship.

The *Investigator* never left the Bay of Mercy. McClure took a sledge party across the strait and left a message under Parry's sandstone "monument". He gave the position of his ship and claimed to have discovered the North-West Passage. But for that bombastic message there would almost certainly have been another major tragedy.

The winter that followed was desperately severe. The men were short of food and lacked candles to give them light. Their health deteriorated fast, not only physically. A seaman and one of the best officers, Wyniatt, went mad.

In the spring McClure made preparations to send out the weakest men by sledge: half of them south to the nearest post of the Hudson's Bay Company, and half of them east to Lancaster Sound, in the hope of meeting a whaler. It was a desperate plan, and dictated by McClure's determination to stay with the ship, along with his fittest men, in the hope that she would be freed and thus enabled to complete the Passage. He did not know of the Belcher expedition.

Just when the sledge parties were ready to start, a man was seen hurrying towards them over the ice. McClure, his nerves at breaking point, demanded, "In God's name, who are you?"

The breathless stranger answered, "I'm Lieutenant Pim, late of the *Herald*, now of the *Resolute*. Captain Kellett is in her at Dealy Island."

His own ship and men excepted, the *Herald* was the last ship McClure had seen, and Kellett the last man with whom he had communicated. Kellett had returned to England to join Belcher's expedition, and one of his sledge parties had found McClure's note on Melville Island.

It was a comparatively short sledge journey to Dealy Island. McClure's relief at being able to hand over his sick men was infinite. But he begged to be allowed to attempt the second part of his plan. This time, however, Captain Kellett's response was clear and definite. When he saw the condition of the "fit" men, he ordered that the *Investigator* be abandoned. She was left in the ice with her colours flying.

Most of her crew spent a number of months on Dealy Island recuperating; but Wyniatt was sent straight on by sledge and put aboard a homeward-bound supply ship. Thus when England learned of the discovery of a North-West Passage, it was from a madman.

Meanwhile Collinson, in the *Enterprise*, was pursuing a voyage that proved more successful in finding evidence of Franklin. To begin with, he followed in the steps of McClure, a season behind him, and, after sailing up Prince of Wales Strait, finding its northern end blocked with ice, and discovering McClure's message claiming discovery of the North-West Passage (Collinson's mate, Murray Parkes, crossed by sledge and foot to Melville Island), he sailed round Banks Island, nearly reached where the *Investigator* was imprisoned, and then turned back to winter on the west coast of Victoria Island.

It was not till late the next season that the *Enterprise* could again continue on her way, and Collinson spent the next winter at Cambridge Bay, in the south-eastern part of Victoria Island. From the Eskimos he met there he obtained a fragment of a door and also an engine bolt. The *Erebus* and *Terror* had been fitted with small auxiliary engines, but Collinson had no interpreter and thus could make no further inquiry. He in fact came quite close to where the ships were held, but found a message in which Rae said that he was searching the area. Turning back to the west, Collinson had to spend another winter in the Arctic before he could clear Bering Strait; and by the time he was back in England, after five years away, it was too late for his findings to be of use.

The reason is that, seven months before the *Enterprise* arrived home, Dr Rae of the Hudson's Bay Company had reported that King William Land was an island; that he had heard from Eskimos of white men struggling southward on foot, dying as they marched, some six years before; and that he had obtained, in the form of crested silverware and Franklin's Order of Merit, unmistakable proof of those men's identity.

When Lord Palmerston's government refused to act on this, Lady Franklin, who had already spent half her fortune on the search, arranged yet another expedition. In the conviction that her husband had discovered the true North-West Passage, she bought the *Fox*, gave her to McClintock to command, and instructed him to search for written records of what had happened.

Every obstacle that the North could muster was put in McClintock's way. Just short of Lancaster Sound the *Fox* was caught in the ice and helplessly carried back down Baffin Bay and Davis Strait for more than a thousand miles. Directly he was freed from this eight-months imprisonment, McClintock turned north again. This time he got through Lancaster Sound, reached Beechey Island, and from there was inspired to follow Franklin's actual course southward down Peel Sound. But it was blocked by ice. He swung about, made the detour to Prince Regent Inlet and tried five times to force a way through Bellot Strait. Thwarted, he wintered and prepared to reach King William Island by sledge journeys in the spring.

McClintock sent his lieutenant, Hobson, to examine the north coast of King William Island, and himself made a clockwise circuit of it, thus conclusively proving its insularity. He realized that the straits to the east and south of the island were the key to the Passage, but did not himself sail it. On the western shore of the island he found a skeleton still partly clad in tatters of naval uniform, then a boat loaded on a sledge with two skeletons and many relics.

Hobson, for his part, found the only written record of what happened. This, a standard Admiralty form on which two messages had been scrawled, one by the leader of a reconnaissance party in 1847, the other by the captain of the *Erebus* a year later, was found with a pile of discarded clothing and equipment in a cairn on James Ross's Victory Point. The date Graham Gore gives for the first wintering, "1846-7", must be an error for 1845-6.

28 of May 1847   H.M. Ships *Erebus* and *Terror* wintered in the ice in Lat. 70° 05′N Long. 98° 23′ W Having wintered in 1846-7 at Beechey Island . . . after having ascended Wellington Channel to Lat. 77° and returned by the West side of Cornwallis Island
  Sir John Franklin commanding the expedition
  All well
  Party consisting of two Officers and six Men left the ships on Monday 24th. May, 1847.

Gm Gore   Lieut
Chas F Des Voeux   Mate

To this was added eleven months later,

April 25, 1848. H M Ships *Terror* and *Erebus* were deserted on the 22nd. April, 5 leagues NNW of this, having been beset since 12th. Sept. 1846. The officers and crews consisting of 105 souls under the Command of Captain F. R. M. Crozier, landed here. . . . Sir John Franklin died on the 11th. June 1847 and the total loss by death in the Expedition has been to this date 9 Officers & 15 Men

F R M Crozier
Captain and Senior Officer

James Fitzjames
Captain H M S Erebus

  and start on tomorrow 26th for Backs Fish River

From this evidence, the various other finds, and accounts given by Eskimos, McClintock was able to piece together the story of what had happened.

Subsequent discoveries have corroborated, and in some respects have enlarged on, McClintock's conclusions, but have not contradicted them.

From the ships imprisoned in Victoria Strait, reconnaissance parties had found the way they ought to have gone—and could not get back to. Marooned in the ice, the crews began to suffer from the enervating curse of scurvy, which as it weakened them weakened their chances of escaping.

So the decision was taken to drag boats over King William Island, ferry across to the estuary of the Great Fish river, and ascend its waterfall infested course. This was physically beyond them and they lacked the technique of sledging which McClintock had developed during the decade of the search. They attempted much too heavy loads. But some of them crossed Simpson Strait to reach the continental shore, the coastal waters of which were known, mainly from Franklin's coastal surveys, to be navigable all the way to Bering Strait.

Chapter 19

Epilogue

Concerning the little-read story of William Baffin, it was suggested that, if his discovery of Lancaster Sound had been followed up, the North-West Passage might have been sailed before the Civil War—before the urgent and well backed era of seventeenth century exploration ended.

This is worth analysing. Ships, as vehicles for navigating ice, did not change much during the following two centuries. They tended to get bigger, but that was a questionable advantage. Their greater resistance was still nothing compared to the infinite power of ice; they were less manoeuvrable and drew more water. Marine engines, which finally made all the difference to ice navigation, did not become efficient until the search was over.

After Baffin's discovery of the mouth of Lancaster Sound in 1615 (twenty-seven years before the Civil War) no British ship other than a whaler went north of Hudson Strait, and whaler captains were not interested in geographical discovery. It only needed one explorer to penetrate the wide, straight waterway of Lancaster Sound to launch a whole series of voyages, with all the backing still available.

Explorers of the seventeenth century still thought of the Passage as a gateway.

That was why Hudson turned southward directly he was through his strait. The hypothetical penetrators of Lancaster Sound would have tended to do the same. The first turn to the left was a cul-de-sac, but the second (Peel Sound) was viable. When Franklin sailed through it he went wrong because he had a chart which gave him false information about the promising bypass round King William Island. A seventeenth-century navigator would have no chart and therefore would have followed his own judgement. He might have reached Simpson Strait, leaving no major obstacle or even difficult choice in the remaining stretch to Bering Strait and the Pacific. A thousand-to-one chance, perhaps; but it could have happened.

Would it have been a good thing?

The navigator would have received great acclaim, but not lasting fame—or not in his generation. The reaction would have been disappointment, as with Columbus but more lastingly. For people were still hoping for a commercial route, and a thousand-to-one chance is not that. It would have proved a pure achievement—before minds were ready to appreciate something of so little practical value.

In the actual course of history, ships followed each other into Hudson Bay, searching for the North-West Passage. Groseilliers and Radisson would have been little more than curiosities but for their promise of a North-West Passage—in fact Cartwright would not have brought them to England. The Hudson's Bay Company might not have been formed at that important moment. Canada would have of course have been developed, but quite likely as a French colony. Conceivably the Russian claim to Alaska, founded on Bering's early-eighteenth-century voyage, might have been maintained more strongly: it was largely because of that voyage that Captain Cook put his nose through Bering Strait. After the Napoleonic war the British Navy would not have played its splendid part in Arctic exploration. Looking back to the beginnings of our maritime history there was never a stronger magnet than the short cut to Cathay. The North-West Passage was a tremendous incentive—so long as it remained unfound.

As soon as it was achieved—as to all practical and moral purposes it was by Franklin and the men who looked for him—then for the British the chapter was finished and they lived on the memory of it. Although the Passage had not actually been sailed through, what Laurence Sterne called a North-West Passage to the intellectual world had been achieved.

Other nationals have sailed the Passage. In 1903–5 the Norwegian Roald Amundsen navigated it from east to west in the *Gjøa*, a cutter-rigged forty-seven ton herring-boat with a petrol engine. He followed Franklin's course as far as King William Island but then used the by-pass round the eastern and southern coasts of the island, by Rae Strait and Simpson Strait. Thereafter he sailed westwards off the continental coast. He experienced hazards due to gales, fogs, a sluggish compass and uncharted waters but no major difficulties. The reason why the voyage took so long was that he spent two winters in Simpson Strait, in the most convenient natural harbour near the Magnetic Pole. He needed to collect scientific data to add substance to the expedition.

In 1923–4 the Danish anthropologist Knud Rasmussen, who specialized in Eskimo customs, made a similar journey by dog sledge, cutting across from Hudson Bay and following the coast. At Starvation Cove, near the mouth of the Great Fish river, he read the burial service over the skeletons of some of Franklin's men. The search for relics of the explorers of the North-West Passage continued until 1936, the most notable finds being made by two Americans, Charles F. Hall in the 1860s and Lieutenant Schwatka in 1880.

By sea the Passage has been made a number of times: thrice by the Canadian Mounted Police schooner *St Roch* and, most spectacularly, by the 153,000 ton oil tanker *Manhattan* in 1969. This great ship, 306 metres in length—twice the size of the biggest liner and 6,000 times larger than Frobisher's *Michael*, barged her way through by Melville Sound and Prince of Wales Strait, picked up by helicopter one barrel of crude Alaskan oil, and returned as she had come to New York. The commercial potentialities of such a voyage may be gauged by the cost of the *Manhattan's* refit and commission—$40 million. Granted it was an experiment comparable with drilling costs, but she only picked up a token cargo because she could not come closer than twenty-five miles to the Alaskan coast.

The idea of carrying oil by submarine was mooted early in this century, such a voyage being proved possible (not the carrying capacity of submarines) by the USS *Seadragon* in 1960. The ancient dream of finding a North-West Passage changed briefly to finding a commercial use for it. But people woke to the reality that pipelines were more practical.

Ice-breakers can make the Passage without much difficulty and nuclear submarines can cruise under the ice. Anyone can now sail the Passage if he thinks it worthwhile, but light aircraft, or motor sledge, or a once-a-year supply ship from the nearest port have proved the best means of local transportation.

The British, who did virtually all the pioneering, have taken no part in this final phase. For them the North-West Passage became history when McClintock returned in 1859 with an adequate description of how Franklin's voyage had ended.

We are richer for the story of the search. Rather than a chapter in our history it has been a paragraph in every chapter since the sixteenth century. The search was made by men of strikingly different character, mainly for commercial purposes, and it finally paid off in the currency of the mind. There was a money reward offered for finding it, but those who first found it got nothing, most of them not even burial—which increases the idealistic value.

"Our dead bodies must tell the tale," wrote Captain Scott. The North-West Passage was the first exploratory achievement for achievement's sake alone. The South Pole was the next. (The North Pole was marred by a false claim, by argument and perhaps by lack of tragedy.) Not until the mid-nineteenth century were intellects ready to accept achievement as adequate in itself. Of course, already, "scientific purposes" were being advanced. But these mean little or nothing to the man in the street, and there are many more men in the streets than off them. We may like to think of ourselves as practical; but we still admire ideals—accomplished with the greatest possible difficulty.

A friend of mine recently flew to the South Pole for lunch. Recounting this incident he mildly complained that the American base was uncomfortably hot, the central heating being too high. The South Pole would mean no more than any other point on the earth but for the story of how it was first attained.

With Mount Everest it is the same. If the expedition in 1922 had reached the summit it would have no more romantic significance than the Matterhorn. Now, with a half-century epic behind it, the first difficulty in climbing the mountain is getting a place in the fixture list. But this queueing only enhances the old story, as does a pilgrimage.

The North-West Passage is similar yet significantly different. It is further behind us, even the attainment, but it existed far longer in our national aspirations. It came into the English mind when England was one of the weakest sea powers and it was achieved with disaster when it was the strongest. The North-West Passage became an evocative phase while the other ways to the Orient did not. It cannot be claimed by Britain, for the first voyage was piloted by an Italian and the final complete passage made by a Norwegian. It is international, as ideals should be. But it was the longest lasting and is the best remembered, the richest in incident, of all exploratory endeavours. It stirred more emotion among more people than reaching for the moon.

Index